Marigold Way

Outstanding Franchise Leadership

Jay Shah

Foundation ❋ Committment ❋ Legacy

❋
marigold
academy

Published by Marigold Way Books 2025

Printed in the United States of America

ISBN-Paperback-979-8-9926018-0-0

ISBN Hardback-979-8-9926018-1-7

ISBN eBook-979-8-9926018-2-4

Author Website: www.marigoldacademy.com

Editing by Jeffrey A. Mangus

www.jeffreymangus.com

Contents

"Emotions and tenacity are how outstanding leaders are born. The higher you want to go, the deeper your foundation needs to be. But fortune favors the bold, so let me ask, how big would you dream if you knew you couldn't fail?"

~ Jay Shah

LEGAL DISCLAIMER AND NOTICE

This publication provides general information and guidance regarding leadership, childcare business operations and franchise opportunities. The author(s) and publisher present this content understanding that they are not providing legal, financial, accounting, or other professional services. Despite our efforts to ensure accuracy and thoroughness, this book should not be used as a substitute for professional consultation.

Readers should seek appropriate professional counsel before implementing any strategies or acting based on this book's content. This information serves as a general guide and does not replace consulting with qualified professionals in legal, accounting, financial, or business matters. Each business situation is unique and may require specialized advice.

This material is strictly for informational purposes only, and nothing contained herein constitutes a solicitation, recommendation, endorsement, or offer to buy or sell any services or business opportunities. The content is general in nature and does not address the specific circumstances of any individual or entity. Users of this information acknowledge that business decisions involve inherent risks, and results may vary significantly based on numerous factors.

Readers assume sole responsibility for evaluating the merits and risks associated with using any information or content provided in this book. The author and publisher make no warranties, express or implied, and shall not be liable for any damage arising from the use of this information. While we have tried to provide accurate and current information, we cannot guarantee its completeness or suitability for any specific purpose.

Foreword

The franchise model enables entrepreneurs to leverage established brands and operational systems instead of building from scratch. Each franchisee embarks on a unique journey to find the right franchise opportunity that aligns with their objectives and capabilities. This discovery process varies significantly among individuals, reflecting their diverse backgrounds and motivations.

For franchise system founders, developing a franchise system requires a transformative shift from business operator to system leader. They must create a model that not only inspires potential franchisees but also supports their success through comprehensive training, operational frameworks, and community building. Building a strong franchise system requires the ability to see the business through the lens of franchisees. The most effective franchisors adopt a servant leadership approach, constantly seeking ways to enhance system efficiency, improve profitability, and strengthen market presence. Their focus extends beyond individual unit operations to building a sustainable network of successful franchisees who can learn from and support each other.

In Marigold Way, founder Jay Shah walks through the founder journey with humility and candor. His focus on building right from the beginning and his desire to create entrepreneurial opportunities for others is clear. But what also comes through is a heartening personal story about his own personal journey to push through doubt and challenges with an unyielding determination to succeed. Jay's entrepreneurial journey from corporate leadership to founding Marigold Academy demonstrates his unwavering commitment to transforming early childhood education. His personal experiences in overcoming obstacles have shaped Marigold Academy's supportive culture, where every decision is made with both children's development and franchisee growth in mind.

At Marigold Academy, Jay has created an infrastructure that provides franchisees with extensive support, from site selection and construction management to ongoing marketing and operational guidance. His hands-on leadership approach ensures franchisees receive personalized attention throughout their journey, while his commitment to continuous system improvement drives innovation across the network.

Jay's thoughtful and introspective approach to building the Marigold franchise system is part of the ethos of the brand. We watch it unfold as it is happening in real-time. It is compelling to take the journey alongside him and watch this engaging entrepreneur launch his unique vision to work with families and other entrepreneurs who share his passion for education. We can't help but cheer him on and want to see him, and his franchisees, succeed!

Alicia Miller

Managing Director, Emergent Growth Advisors

Phase I. Foundation

Introduction:

A Newfound Leadership Journey-The Marigold Way

*"All good men and women must take responsibility to create legacies that will take the next generation to a level we could only imagine." ~**Jim Rohn***

In 1989, the Education Station Day Care Center in Bloomfield, New Jersey, was the home of a small childcare center for children. Unknown and ordinary, the business was doing well, but serendipitously, the school caught our attention. My wife and I weren't sure why, but we saw potential in that school. We saw a vision, an esteemed American institution, and that school represented something more… our American Dream.

In 2017, we were blessed with twin daughters who inspired the dream of our new business. As professionals in the workforce, we sought the best childcare center, one rich in instruction and child development. One by one, we looked for a childcare center where our children weren't just a number. In our minds, childcare needed to be a second home, but none measured up. Since we could not find what we were looking for, something clicked, and our childcare adventure began.

Today, after acquiring the Education Station in 2019, we transformed it into Marigold Academy, an elite childcare academy with a unique focus on holistic education and child development. We believed that other parents shared our vision, so we created an environment that fosters children's growth in a supportive, loving, and positive atmosphere. When we took over, we were novices in managing a top-tier childcare center, but our passion for creating a special place for children, one that leaves a true legacy of growth and prosperity, was unwavering. Our commitment to helping children thrive and lead fulfilling lives, rather than just being in front of a screen, is what sets us apart.

Our curriculum stood out from the rest, offering children the opportunity to engage in programs like literacy, math, science, music, foreign languages, and even sign language. My wife and I saw our program as a springboard for children, promoting diversity and appreciating different cultures and beliefs. Inspired by our desire as parents, we wanted to give children of all ages every chance to help them along the way.

As parents, we know children are like sponges, absorbing everything around them. Unfortunately, some of what they are absorbing is not good. Since opening Marigold Academy, we have recognized, as individuals and as a society, that we must challenge our children, providing rich nutrients to their minds and bodies for their growth while promoting intense curiosity for learning.

Today, imagine our schools in Randolph and Bloomfield, New Jersey, filled with memories of lives lived to the fullest, gentle reminders of pushing against all odds. As I sit here, I'm surrounded by small recaps of my journey to become the CEO of Marigold Academy.

Looking back at my life and tracing the path that led me to where I am today, it is impossible not to be overwhelmed with gratitude. But as a leader, I have recognized the need to give back and help others succeed, leaving behind a transcending legacy. My name is Jay Shah, and I am an Indian American immigrant. As I write this book, it is the story of sacrifice, unwavering determination, and my leadership journey, embracing my heritage and upbringing while striving for success in America.

It all started with my parents, who dreamed of more and knew that coming to America was the opportunity our family needed. My father, an accounting executive in India, a man of few words but immense ambition and emotion, dreamed of a life beyond the boundaries of our small city in India. My mother, a stay-at-home parent in India and a woman of true, fearless inspiration, was ready to dedicate the rest of her life to better the lives of her children. With hearts filled with hope and determination, our family left behind everything we knew to pursue the elusive American Dream. My parents' unyielding commitment to providing a better future for our family was nothing short of inspiring. It struck me in the heart.

In May 1995, as our family embarked on our journey from India to America, we encountered countless challenges along the way. Settling in Canton, Michigan, everything hit us. Language barriers loomed, making simple tasks like ordering a meal or asking for directions impossible. For me, being fifteen, I had a mountain of problems. Entering high school in tenth grade, I couldn't speak the language; I dressed funny and not cool or hip like the other children. Other children picked on me and teased me relentlessly. It was tough. I couldn't speak their language but faced it each day, never backing down. But my father's resilience was one of courage. His eagerness and willingness to adapt to our new home propelled him forward. His actions inspired me as he immersed himself in American culture to overcome this obstacle and embrace his new home.

Meanwhile, my mother faced her own struggles. When she arrived, she had to get a job, something she had never done before. It was tough for her because she had no actual work skills. She dedicated her whole life to being a housewife and mother. It was all she knew. But, with no hesitancy, she followed my father, stepping up and getting a job in an automotive factory along with him. My father, a banking executive, made a sacrifice as they thrust him into manual labor, working with his hands and assembling automotive parts. It was a significant step down; working for minimum wage and doing something he was overqualified to do. He never complained. Never.

Growing up, I took to heart all of this and now see my parents' sacrifices, which were not just for themselves but for the future they envisioned for me and my sister. As I have lived my life, this alone has been my cornerstone: the ability to sacrifice and put one's needs below another's. They instilled in us the values of hard work, determination, and the importance of education. Their unwavering commitment to these principles became the foundation upon which I have built my life and business.

I worked multiple jobs, attended night classes, and filled my days with studying, homework, and work. There wasn't room for anything else. And when you're starting out, it takes this kind of dedication to see any success. I embraced the value of education and threw myself into my studies, determined to make the most of America's opportunities. However, during those late nights of studying, I understood the value of commitment and had to dig deep to persevere. There were days when I would come home after a long day of work and university classes, feeling defeated. But I never once thought of giving up. I knew that every sacrifice I made would be worth it in the end. Oddly, during these times of difficulty and struggle, I found perseverance and determination, which became the driving force behind my career pursuit. I embraced the value of tenacity and grit to make the most of America's opportunities.

In his book *Leaders Eat Last*, Simon Sinek said, "You must pivot, change direction, and do the one thing you were meant to do, inspiring others along the way." This has been what I've aspired to do: helping others be the best they can be. As leaders, my wife and I saw that skilled and trained staff and teachers were essential, so we developed a plan to provide unlimited growth opportunities. Our philosophy is that a teacher's desired growth should be based on merit, hard work, and strong work ethics, not on their status, education, or circumstance. We wanted to help others achieve their dreams through essential leadership principles, which I intend to share with you, putting you on the right course for long-term success.

I have broken this book into three phases, starting with Phase One, *Foundation*, which will describe how to use your life experiences as a springboard for pushing yourself as a leader. You will understand the importance of knowing your WHY and purpose. Here, you will learn how to succeed by stepping outside your comfort zone and developing a positive mindset for growth. You will have the tools to gain clarity and learn how to use failure as feedback to climb the business ladder toward outstanding leadership.

In this phase, you will understand the importance of overcoming your fears of leaping into a new career or a new opportunity. I will give you solid leadership principles and real-world tools to change and make a better life for you and your family.

However, it won't be easy. You must be strong, open your mind, and promise to act by applying the principles for anything to work. You must prepare to get moving—without fear of changing—and step into your new career. There aren't any shortcuts. There isn't any magic pill. The knowledge and methods I describe here will help you learn to be an exceptional leader and excel in whatever field you plan to enter.

In *Marigold Way* Phase Two, *Commitment,* you will learn how to leverage your current professional and personal relations to further your business and leadership. I will explain using an invisible marketing machine and professional networking through relationships to develop business and profitability in the long term. To be an outstanding leader, you must recognize the power of knowing your Zone of Genius and your Must-Haves, which we will explore in great detail.

Throughout history, countless individuals have left indelible marks on society through their commitment to their dreams and dedication to hard work. But none of them got there because they did not know their WHY and Must-Haves. From prominent leaders like Mahatma Gandhi and Martin Luther King Jr. to innovators like Thomas Edison and Steve Jobs, their legacies remind us of the power of perseverance and knowing their direction as they aspired for greatness.

In Phase Three, *Legacy,* you learn the secrets surrounding genuine success: empowering others to reach their full potential. Inspired by my parents' actions and the examples set by prominent leaders, I dreamed bigger. I desired to make a difference on a grand scale and leave a lasting imprint on the world. I understood that to accomplish this, I had to pursue the expertise needed to help others. With this book, *Marigold Way,* I will set you on the path to a rewarding career and an outstanding life by sharing every moment that has led me to succeed and leave a living legacy behind.

When I look back at my father's sacrifice, leaving an executive status for a minimum wage labor job, he believed that genuine success lay not in personal wealth or material possessions but in leaving behind a long-standing legacy that would inspire future generations. And my father indeed left behind a legacy that will forever inspire me.

Despite the initial hardships, my parents never wavered in their commitment to building a better life for our family. They worked tirelessly, often taking on multiple shifts to make ends meet and ensure we had every opportunity available. Through their unwavering dedication, they not only achieved their version of the American Dream, but also laid the foundation for my future success.

I followed their path, working multiple jobs, leaping into new careers, and opening doors I never would have opened. Despite what many around me thought, I followed my entrepreneurial spirit with everything I had, never giving up and ensuring I found the one thing I wanted to do for the rest of my life. You will, too. You will learn about the vital aspects of using the power of a solid mindset to advance your career and business.

Here, I will take you through the triumphs and tribulations of my family's immigrant experience, providing a glimpse into our challenges while building a life in America. From moments of cultural clash, to pursuing higher education, to taking a leap of faith and pursuing an entrepreneurial journey, each step of our journey has taught us valuable lessons about resilience, determination, and the importance of embracing our roots. I will share it all, but this story is not just about my family's journey; it reflects the broader experience, sacrifices, and triumphs of many others to add leadership success.

As a new leader, you will understand that success is a testament to the resilience and determination that one must undergo to navigate a new business and career. As you embark on this leadership journey, reflect on the values and experiences that have shaped you. Embrace your heritage by self-introspection on who you are, what you are made of, and where you want to go. This is where legacy begins.

Benjamin Disraeli once said, "The legacy of heroes is the memory of a great name and the inheritance of a great example." So, I welcome you and encourage you to take one of the first steps in changing your life, setting an excellent example for your future and family. As you read *Marigold Way*, I hope you walk away filled with newfound knowledge, encouragement, and the superpower leading to your major success. It's all here at your fingertips, and the energy is palpable—I thank you for joining me in this melting pot of ideas, experiences, and methods that will allow you to expand your world and live the American Dream.

Chapter 1:

Knowing your WHY and Purpose

"It doesn't matter how strong your why is; if what you are offering is not solving a problem, it won't be impactful or have a lasting legacy." ~ **Jay Shah**

My father was a chief accountant in the City of Detroit. He poured his heart and soul into the job, dedicating a significant portion of his life to his passion, until he was abruptly let him go in 2004. He was fifty-eight. The City of Detroit was in big trouble with the ballooning pension fund and corruption. As a result, the city could no longer honor its obligations, causing everything to collapse. Despite being a dedicated and an outstanding employee, losing his job was crippling. As a result, my father felt devastated, and the emotional toll became too much for him, causing him to break down. I had never seen him like this before. It hit hard. As a son, I looked up to my father and tried to follow in his footsteps. His work ethic. The ethics he upholds. All his values were inspiring. The sight of him at the end of his rope, helpless... it scarred me. He had always prospered and thrived, never complaining about his work and doing everything he could to provide for our family. After the layoff, he was the picture of despair and loss. The city of Detroit had financial troubles, and my father, being a higher-up, got the axe.

For the first time in my life, I realized the importance of controlling your destiny and being your own boss, never wanting to be a victim of a job loss. As luck would have it, following the layoff of my father, I got my first job out of engineering school. As a family, we achieved balance. However, engineering was not my calling, and I realized my genuine passion for financial management and operations. To secure a job in financial services, I pursued a Master of Business Administration from Michigan State University in 2007. Upon finishing my MBA, I switched careers to pursue my passion for financial services.

I joined Ally Bank during the banking crisis in 2008; this was the worst time in the financial services industry. In 2009, because of the banking system meltdown and ongoing recession, Ally Bank started experiencing financial problems. To survive, the bank had laid off one-third of its staff, which included me. Just like my father, I became a casualty of the recession. My income was in the six figures, which was gone when they dropped the hammer. It was my second wake-up call, showing me that there was another way: I must never depend on others and never be a casualty of life.

... A life-changing seed was sown.

The challenge was that no one in our family had ever tried to own or start their own business. There was no such belief in doing something like that; if anything, our family frowned upon it. Growing up, our family was like millions of others, following what many call The American Dream: Go to school. Get educated. Go to college. Graduate. Get a job. Work until you retire and fade away while raising a family. My family and circles feared entrepreneurship and going against the norm.

... I had other plans.

With family and achieving greatness, my parents had left their comfortable lives behind. They stepped out of their comfort zone to pursue their Why, which was to create an environment where their children could thrive and build their personal legacies. Even if that meant taking a minimum-wage menial job working on an assembly line to fulfill their purpose, they did it humbly. Following their footsteps, I stepped out of my comfort zone. I pursued my more significant purpose of owning a business, building a legacy, providing for my family, and being an outstanding and influential leader in my community. It was my purpose.

It all happened seven years ago when I discovered my passion for working in early childhood education. I found my desire to help families and children. It set me on an alternative career path, leading me to own and grow Marigold Academy. But following my passion didn't come easy.

Leadership is a combination of skills, mindset, knowledge, perseverance, and a bit of serendipitous luck. Taking advantage of opportunities and being open to them is all it takes. Everyone who has had success has reached their status with some luck, but the key is creating opportunities for luck to strike by being out there, going after what you want, and being driven. Without opportunity and drive to succeed, luck cannot happen.

After months of searching and evaluating other childcare centers, my wife and I found a subpar side to the childcare industry. We saw the ways not to do things. It was eye-opening, and we knew we were on a mission to improve things and make a colossal impact. After months of searching for a center, we found the Education Station Childcare Center, and everything came into focus.

After serving the community for over thirty years, the owner was retiring from educating local youngsters. I drove two hours to see the center, and it was perfect as I stepped inside the center. It was one of the happiest and most positive childcare centers I've ever seen. The teachers and children all smiled ear to ear; the center and playground were amazing, and the location was perfect. As clear as day, I saw the vision that would soon become Marigold Academy.

***

Vignette: Note from Kruti Shah

Marigold Academy, from the first day, has been a place that is open to opportunities for teachers and other people who are passionate about childcare. That is a milestone and a must-have for us, as our staff is passionate about working with children. It is crucial that we know their heart is in it. We always consider the quality of education and the childcare the children will receive. We also emphasize the importance of supporting and hiring qualified staff.

***

Our mission was clear after we bought the center. We never intended to create a school where it turns into a baby-sitting operation, where children are in front of screens all day. By renovating the center, we created a healthier learning environment for teachers and children, and an aesthetically pleasing environment for parents seeking a safe and vibrant environment for their children.

The concepts we introduced were advanced enrichment programs, such as phonics, STEM, and foreign and sign languages. The emphasis was on promoting diversity and inclusion. Seeing the vision and following our WHY, we stepped up, learning and listening to the staff and voices of the families, taking what we learned to develop a top-tier curriculum and enriching environment.

We created a philosophy that empowers teachers because cultivating happy teachers means happy children, and happy children means happy parents. That became the Marigold philosophy that is deeply rooted in our culture and everything we do. We wanted to create an environment where teachers and staff were at the forefront. This is a fundamental principle. The best teachers make the best students. It was our destiny and our legacy. My WHY and purpose were coming into focus.

***

Every one of us is fighting a battle to know who we are, what our WHY is, and what our purpose is. In his book *Find Your Why: A Practical Guide for Discovering Your Purpose for Your and Your Team*, Simon Sinek said, "There are two ways to build a career or business. We can go through life hunting and pecking, looking for opportunities, hoping for something to connect. Or we can go through life with intention, knowing what our peace looks like, knowing our WHY, and going straight to the places we fit."

What is your WHY and intent? What is your purpose in life?

Have you ever given it some thought? You should because it doesn't matter who you are, where you are from, or what you do. Knowing your WHY is vital to achieving success in anything you do. Your WHY is the purpose for which you exist, inspiring you to do what you want for your family, children, loved ones, and community. Your why is at the heart of everything you aspire to do.

Motivational expert Tony Robbins understood the importance of this. From an early age, he grew up in a turbulent family riddled with financial insecurity, his parents' unhealthy relationship putting him in an arduous situation. Robbins talks about his "watershed moment" when he attended a session by motivational speaker Jim Rohn. Inspired by Rohn's teachings, Robbins changed his life. At 17, he took control of his fate and began a journey of self-discovery and empowerment.

His WHY became clear, and his transformation started with small yet significant actions, such as saving money from his job as a janitor to attend personal development seminars. These experiences ignited his life's purpose to help others unlock their full potential and achieve lasting fulfillment. It became his life's WHY and purpose.

Knowing your WHY requires self-introspection and isn't a run-of-the-mill buzzword or business trend. It's a fundamental pillar of success, guiding your decisions and the driver showing you direction and purpose. But how do you find your WHY? Here is a hint. Your job title, salary, or skills are only some of the essential things. There is more.

The key lies in being open to opportunity, humbling oneself to see the bigger picture, and understanding the core values and principles that make you who you are. Author Mark Twain said, "The two most important days in your life are the day you are born and the day you find out why." As an aspiring leader, discover your true "Why" by questioning what brings you joy. How do you see yourself spending the remainder of your life? What makes you feel fulfilled? What kind of impact would you like to leave on this world? When you align your work with what affects you, success becomes a natural byproduct of your pursuit, and you can open unforeseen doors.

In 2021, new doors opened for my wife and me as we spotted another opportunity to expand Marigold Academy's reach by acquiring a second school. When we bought the center, it was a struggling operation right from the start. We needed new staff to implement our systems, redesign the core curriculum, and increase enrollment. Determined, following our WHY and proven strategy, we hired caring new staff and improved the center and curriculum to match the high standards we believe in.

By pursuing our vision, we put in the effort to turn the new center into a thriving childcare center, offering top-notch care and a comprehensive curriculum and prioritizing the well-being of our children and teachers. In that new center, we have since raised revenue by nearly three times and profitability by five times in just a few years, which is a testament and affirmation of following your purpose.

That turnaround highlights the effectiveness of our compassionate approach and business acumen. Following our WHY, it was our calling. We started Marigold Academy franchise for three main reasons:

Empowering Children and Parents.

After touring other childcare institutions, I knew we were on the right path by providing exceptional quality care, an engaging curriculum, immaculate facilities, and supporting the team's commitment to nurturing each child. At Marigold Academy, our caregivers do more than supervise; they enrich children's lives by providing warmth and one-on-one instruction, allowing them to flourish. And for parents, our staff works to educate their children in a respected and safe environment, giving them genuine peace of mind.

Because raising thriving children starts early, now more than ever, dual-income families need reliable, nurturing care they can trust. At Marigold Academy, we ensure that parents can pursue their careers with peace of mind, knowing their children will never be neglected. With a high demand for childcare that feels like family, Marigold aims to have a center in every community where locals can entrust their little ones to grow with us in an environment that feels like home.

Empower Staff to Build Their Personal Legacies.

What drives me most about franchising is seeing our talented staff members grow and advance in their careers. Every day, I rely on my passion for franchising because it is an opportunity to help our outstanding employees thrive. Marigold Academy employs fifty-five staff members whose passion and dedication to early childhood education amaze me daily. Now, franchising creates new career ladders for our driven staff members in operations, training, customer service, and more. Their years of nurturing children make them perfect for encouraging new franchisees to deliver Marigold's brand of care.

Upward career mobility through franchising means crafting professional legacies by sharing Marigold's values more widely. Seeing familiar faces advance through the ranks is our WHY and purpose as we expand our footprint. We are expanding opportunities for the loyal team members who put their heart and soul into Marigold's vision daily. Their personal growth is Marigold's legacy and my success as a leader.

Paying the Mentorship Forward.

I've discovered that many dedicated professionals share my dream of building a family legacy through business ownership. Yet, leaping from a corporate career feels daunting without guidance. I meet countless incredible community members who feel stuck—unsure how to transform their commitment and passion into an enriching business opportunity.

My journey held all the same doubts before Marigold showed me the way. Now, paying that mentorship forward is my purpose. We aim to cultivate the next generation of compassionate business leaders who will serve local families and own a rewarding business while making a positive difference.

With Marigold, it isn't a pipe dream; you take the first step forward with the right guide to show the way. Yet, how important is it for a new franchisee to know their WHY and purpose? It is critically important that you align with Marigold's mission, understanding that Marigold Academy extends beyond superior early education and care, as we intend to empower children to prosper, enrich young lives, and nurture career growth and fulfillment for our teachers and staff.

***

Finding your "WHY" is not linear, but more about growth and evolution. Because your WHY and purpose may shift over time, allow yourself to adapt and refine your "WHY" as needed. Pay attention because knowing your WHY is where the real magic happens and is only the beginning. It unlocks peak performance, driving the meaning behind your work.

Your WHY provides clarity and direction, giving balance to your life. Yet, when WHY is absent, balance cannot happen. Your WHY acts as an inner compass so you can focus your efforts on what matters most. Without it, you're lost. Simon Sinek, author of *Start with Why*, said, "Everything falls into place when we know WHY we do what we do. When we do not, we have to push things into place."

This resonated with me because I know that connecting to your WHY stops feeling like "work," and you look forward to it every morning. Before you or your business can have a positive impact, you must know why you're doing it. It must be clear and come down to this: to separate yourself from the rest, focus on WHY you do what you do, not just what you do. I have found several ways to see and know your WHY. Let's explore.

Explore Your Childhood.

Look at what captured your curiosity, interests, natural strengths, and clues about who you wanted to become. Your youngest self often had the drive and stirring of what you wanted before external influences, such as society, friends, families, and relationships, have shaped you.

Reminisce about significant life events, decisions, and pivotal points that, over time, reveal patterns about what emotionally moves you.

Examine the positive motivations and seminal life moments where you saw yourself doing that one thing. What did you daydream about? Sports? Music? Education? Whatever that is, how did it make you feel? Reminiscing on your childhood memories could include your heroes and how they affected your life. What were their heroic sparks and values that have shaped your motivational patterns? Who were your childhood heroes, and how did they affect you?

One Year to Live Method.

One method I've used is asking, "If I had a year left to live, what would I want to do?" What would that one thing be for you? Envision your last 365 days and how and why you would spend them. Also, it is crucial to assess your current role and deeply examine your feelings about whether it fulfills or drains you. Look at your feelings as motivation, strength, passion, and purpose as frameworks.

What is Your Legacy?

Another avenue is to ask yourself, what would you want your legacy to be? What problems do you want to solve in your life and for others? How can you be effective in doing what compels you? Whose lives do you want to affect? What fires you up? What interests you, and is the one thing that will keep you focused for hours?

Sir Winston Churchill said, "There comes a special moment in everyone's life for which that person was born. That special opportunity, when he seizes it, will fulfill his mission—a mission for which he is qualified. In that moment, he will find greatness. It is his finest hour."

We do not have to look far to see the many notable individuals who figured out their WHY, followed it and found outstanding success.

Jeff Bezos, founder of Amazon, is a prime example. Bezos dedicated himself to delivering the best user experience across the Amazon platform. But what caused this success? He understood his WHY and value for himself and the company: the vision to pioneer superior commerce powered by people and technology. Bezos said, "We see our customers as guests to a party, and we are the hosts. It's our daily job to make every important aspect of the customer experience a little bit better."

Knowing Your Purpose.

Nelson Mandela once said, "There is no passion to be found playing small, in settling for a life less than the one you are capable of living." He was right. If you don't know your purpose, create one. Understanding your purpose sets you apart, affecting your world and career.

The renowned philosopher Ralph Waldo Emerson said, "The world makes way for the man who knows where he is going. What lies behind you and what lies in front of you pales compared to what lies inside of you."

Uncovering your purpose must be with intention. Having a clear sense of purpose drives your actions and attracts opportunities along with like-minded individuals who share in your vision in business and life. American author Mark Twain once said, "Keep away from people who try to belittle your ambitions. Small people always do that, but the great ones make you feel that you, too, can become great." Be active with others that mirror your morals and values any chance you get. Surround yourself with those who inspire and uplift you; their stories can guide and shed light on your journey. You never know who you will encounter and how that one interaction will change your life.

Through a similar process, I came across some of the most significant individuals in my life. They each had a purpose. I've found that seeking inspiration from others who have walked similar paths is a way to grow and develop. Turning to mentors, coaches, and successful individuals is the intelligent way to find fulfillment in your business endeavors and personal lives.

***

The WHY of Marigold Academy Franchising

Leading with your "WHY" as a new Marigold Academy franchisee leader can inspire staff loyalty by focusing on programs to uplift staff and offering exemplary services to stand out in your industry. By fostering a deep emotional connection with the staff and families you serve, the approach allows you and your franchise to differentiate beyond other childcare centers, creating a meaningful impact that transcends traditional business strategies. As a leader and franchisee, have the courage to embrace failure and setbacks. See every stumble as a chance for meaningful growth and self-discovery.

Defining success on your terms is essential to better understanding your purpose. Motivational expert Gary Vaynerchuk said, "Purpose is what your life is about, not what your job is about." Society often imposes expectations and definitions of success upon us, but true fulfillment comes from aligning our actions with our unique values and aspirations.

As Steve Jobs once advised, "You have limited time. Don't waste it living someone else's life." Take the time to reflect on what matters to you and define what success means to you personally. By defining success on your terms, you can navigate your path with clarity and purpose.

Start by setting clear goals that align with your values and passions. Break them down into actionable steps and create a roadmap for yourself. Remember, as American business magnate Warren Buffett advised, "The best investment you can make is in yourself." Invest in your personal and professional growth by acquiring new skills, seeking opportunities for learning and development, and taking calculated risks. Stay calm and allow yourself the necessary time, as uncovering your purpose is a process, not an endpoint.

Your life's goal is to discover and commit to your purpose. Whether it be business, family, or anything. So, embrace self-discovery and allow yourself the space to evolve and grow. To find your WHY and purpose, change your mindset, approach each day with an open mind, and be ready to learn and adapt.

As Marigold Academy adapts to novel approaches in childcare, our WHY and purpose are clear. Marigold Academy can expand nationwide by providing outstanding early childhood development and fostering local jobs. Marigold Academy's blend of educational excellence and sound business practices has the potential to become a gold-standard brand for entrepreneurs and parents across the country. The demand for the high-quality care we deliver has never been higher. It is our mission and purpose.

Trust that your purpose will unfold as you align your actions with your values. Remember that understanding your purpose in business and life requires introspection, inspiration from others, resilience, defining success on your terms, meaningful conversations, and decisive actions. Embrace the process, stay true to yourself, and let your purpose and WHY guide you toward a fulfilling and meaningful life.

***

Important Points

- Finding your WHY is about being open to opportunity, humbling yourself to see the bigger picture, and understanding the core values that drive your actions.

- Understanding your WHY and purpose is about knowing who you are and what you stand for.

- To uncover your authentic "WHY," as an aspiring leader, ask yourself: What brings you happiness? What makes you feel fulfilled? What impact do you want to make in this world?

- When you align your work with what has an impact, success becomes a natural byproduct of your pursuit.

Chapter 2:

Getting Out of Your
Comfort Zone

"Life begins at the end of your comfort zone."
~ Neale Donald Walsch

In December 1917, the Wright brothers changed aviation with the first of four flights of a prototype aircraft they believed could fly. Defying expectations and pursuing their dreams, they accomplished human flight, lasting 12 seconds and covering only 180 feet. But proving it wasn't a fluke or streak of luck, the last flight traveled over 852 ft. in 59 seconds.

It was a monumental moment, as the brothers had solved the mystery of powered flight. Yet those historical flights were over two men trying to do the impossible. This is a story of Orville and Wilbur Wright getting out of their comfort zone, pushing the limits, doing the unimaginable, overcoming doubt and naysayers, and diving deep into the unknown.

As a leader, I have faced challenges throughout my career, where I had to embrace discomfort to advance myself and my career. Getting into the childcare space, an industry my wife and I knew nothing about, the idea was uncomfortable for us. It was scary. It was one of the most challenging decisions we ever had to make, and it required unwavering commitment and getting out of my comfort zone. I felt an unwavering belief in my cause, fueled by determination, perseverance, and resilience.

I was still walking into an unknown, which wasn't comfortable. Driven by my purpose, I stepped up, knowing I had to learn everything about childcare while putting my family's financial well-being on the line. We wanted to create an enriching and empowering environment for children in all communities.

Our journey with Marigold Academy took us out of our physical comfort zone. Our family had to move from Pennsylvania to New Jersey. It was a monumental step, leaving our comfortable home filled with memories. Yet, we had to be close to our new business, even though we had spent the last ten years building our lives in Pennsylvania with friends and family.

Our children were born in that house, and our home had sentimental values that we still hold in our hearts. We had roots there, making moving away scary. But our drive and passion for Marigold Academy were too strong, and we couldn't ignore it, so tough decisions had to be made. After careful consideration, we followed our higher purpose, getting far removed from our comfort zone to achieve the greatness we aspired to achieve.

As Marigold Academy grew in reputation and as a company, franchising our system was an idea that came to the forefront. When I decided to franchise Marigold Academy, I was excited and started consulting with industry experts to launch the concept. Then reality hit hard. It was a wake-up call about how much time and money it would take and the immense sacrifice I'd make for my family. I knew it would result in less time spent with my wife and children, and it would come with a lot of risk. In my own thoughts, I realized that I already have two well-established and highly successful schools. Being in a comfort zone, I had financial security and an ideal work-life balance. My nerves got the best of me, leading me to abandon the project. However, for the next nine months, there wasn't a single day when I did not think about franchising Marigold Academy to reach more communities.

My *WHY* and *purpose* were my calling. It burned inside the thoughts of how franchising could change my life and the lives of many others, including the next generation of entrepreneurs. I reached the point where I could not bear to live with "what if" any longer. Not deciding to franchise and testing the waters was something I couldn't go into old age thinking or regretting. Refusing to quit, I was determined to see it through. So, stepping out of my comfort zone, I consulted and discussed with my wife where my heart was and what kind of financial commitment and personal sacrifices it would take to make my dream a reality. And my understanding wife, stepping away from her comfort zone, obliged and pushed me to go with my gut and shoot for my dreams.

We all seek safety, stability, and order in our lives. This is our comfort zone — familiar patterns, habits, and routines. Even our social circles, environments, and thought processes become comfortable and normal. While reassuring, staying in our comfort zones limits ourselves to new ideas and ways to improve our lives.

By getting out of your comfort zone, you can rewire beliefs, expose your thinking to challenges, and develop your potential for growth. Unfortunately, profound change and fulfillment often exist far beyond what our comfort zones permit.

Prior to Marigold Academy, I was in a senior finance position, making six figures with a clear path for upward mobility in my corporate career. When I stepped away cold to pursue my dream of enriching the lives of young children and building Marigold Academy, the idea was not for the faint of heart. Being human, I had doubts, but my desire to achieve and make something stood the test of time. A legacy for me and my family was more significant, pushing me to find success.

As a dreamer and aspiring leader, you must do this in your career and life. You must walk away from your comfort zone to reach new heights. There are no shortcuts to getting out of your comfort zone; only hard work, grit, and tenacity can achieve your dreams. The only way to do this is to step out and embrace the discomfort to better yourself and your family.

Discomfort is a frame of mind, and you must reframe into a new perspective. Accepting discomfort unlocks next-level versions of who we can become and influences how we show up for others in our lives. If we resist change, we shortchange ourselves. On the one hand, the inner conflict arises from the tension between staying comfortable, and discomfort and taking risks. One part of the conflict involves taking bold risks, while the other part is filled with insecurities that hold us back. The only way to find balance is through understanding who we are as leaders and individuals. Once you find balance, both parts will lead to more informed and solid decisions and personal and professional advancement.

Discomfort serves as a sign of progress and an opportunity for breakthroughs. The author of the book *The Light of the Heart*, Roy T. Bennett, said, "You never change your life until you step out of your comfort zone; change begins at the end of your comfort zone." Change is the excellent product of getting past your comfort zone. Push hard past your boundaries, and you'll have many opportunities to bolster your confidence in situations you might have previously felt afraid of.

According to a study published in the *Journal of Positive Psychology*, individuals who embrace discomfort as a natural part of growth are more likely to achieve their goals and experience higher levels of well-being. As renowned author and speaker Brené Brown put it, "Vulnerability is not winning or losing; it has the courage to show up and be seen when we have no control over the outcome." By embracing discomfort, we open ourselves up to the possibility of failure and more tremendous success and growth.

Failure is uncomfortable. That is a fact. But, as a leader, you will face failure on many levels. However, embracing failure as feedback separates the outstanding leaders from the pack. Taking what you learn from failure and using it to take the following steps is vital. Overcoming any failure means understanding it, getting out of your comfort zone, and creating a solution addressing the failure. Failure is an important feedback tool for learning. As an aspiring leader, you can use failure to ask questions, gather information, and improve.

Humility and inner strength are traits found in the world's most outstanding leaders. Overcoming pride is challenging, but it's the only path to professional growth by embracing failure as feedback. Otherwise, you'll be stuck and not make any progress.

With leadership, stepping away from your comfort zone can be intimidating. John C. Maxwell stated, "Growth is not automatic; it requires stepping out of our comfort zones." Our world thrives on progress and change, and if you cannot embrace personal and professional growth, you may miss valuable opportunities. According to recent statistics, individual leaders who seek growth and step out of their comfort zones are 30% more likely to advance professionally than their stagnant counterparts. Stepping away from everyday routines and mindsets, they enhance individual potential and lay a solid foundation for meaningful leadership and a legacy.

So, how can you step out of your comfort zone as a new leader? It starts with understanding where, how, and *why* you are avoiding what's uncomfortable. Humans have a natural instinct to avoid discomfort, which has been crucial for survival throughout history. However, understanding why we avoid discomfort is the first step to overcoming it. Self-awareness is the foundation of effective leadership, and it's rarely simple to achieve, but crucial for wielding influence.

Self-awareness is your superpower for getting out of your comfort zone as you recognize and understand your thoughts, emotions, behaviors, and actions. It is essential for self-improvement, personal growth, and emotional intelligence. Self-awareness helps you gain control over your actions and improve your overall situation and effectiveness as a leader.

Here are some practical tips to help you as a leader understand and embrace discomfort:

Set Clear Goals: Set achievable goals that push you slightly beyond your comfort zone. These goals should be specific, measurable, attainable, relevant, and time-bound (SMART). Sit down and take the time to explore yourself and what you want to do and achieve. What are the most important things you want to see happen with your life and your business?

My wife and I sat down and wrote out what we saw as pros and cons with our first Marigold Academy. We developed a plan of execution that improved the lives of parents, staff, and children. We weeded out any flaws, focusing on what works for everyone involved.

Network Is Your Net Worth: Network with people who possess expertise in the areas of your interest. Seek fresh social circles to gain exposure to diverse perspectives that challenge assumptions. Study the people who have walked a similar path you want to embark on.

Raise your hand, ask questions, seek help. Pushing past shyness builds courage each time.

Develop your support systems and identify trusted advisors, friends, coaches, or professionals you can seek counsel from if facing decisions. Bill Gates, founder of Microsoft, once said, "Everyone needs a coach. It doesn't matter whether you're a basketball player, a tennis player, a gymnast, or a bridge player."

Take a 30-day Challenge: Step away from your comfort zone by setting monthly goals and pushing the limits through extra activities, environments, or exposures. Record and document what you've gleaned, and by trusting yourself to pursue those directions, you will build strong self-trust in your decision-making with many unknowns.

Micro Adventures. Say Yes: To further expand past your comfort zone, take micro-adventures. Small daily and weekly adventures to find the magic and inspiration in and around you are vital. Much like the movie *Yes Man* with Jim Carrey, instead of saying no to new opportunities, say yes and watch new unforeseen opportunities come your way. By saying yes, you open yourself up to the unknown and possible. Doing this involves you in new things, often bringing humility, a positive trait that is one of the best to have as a newfound leader.

Seeking Solitude: Steve Jobs said, "Take some time to be alone. Not to be lonely, but to be alone with your thoughts. It's the only way to create something great." While solitude may not be comfortable for everyone, it is the necessary route to discovering one's true self as a person and a leader. Being with yourself in a place with no distractions will refresh your mind and spirit, opening new thoughts and fresh directions.

Meditate. Spend time with yourself by carving out time in your day to connect with your inner self. Put yourself first. In our society today, with constant social media distraction and noise, finding intimate connections is challenging. Purposeful solitude lets us rethink old stories about ourselves. Silence shifts us from tiring routines to rediscovering inspiration. Quiet spaces we fear often overflow with creative potential. Alone time in quiet reflection can spark powerful insights and direction.

With direction and influence, listening to that inner voice will not steer you wrong. Let it be your north star and foundation to overcome resistance to change. Overcoming your resistance to change, you need to take small steps. Doing so makes you more comfortable with discomfort, and gradually, you can increase the difficulty level and challenge yourself. There is no growth in comfort and no vision in the familiar. We don't discover new things by staying comfortable. Trying bold things off the beaten path lets us learn and grow.

***

Important Points

- You must walk away from your comfort zone to reach new heights.

- Setting clear and achievable goals will push you beyond your comfort zone.

- Your network is your net worth. Your connections and relationships in both personal and professional spheres are invaluable assets that can open doors to opportunities, provide support, and contribute significantly to your overall success and growth potential.

- The only way to know who you are as a person and a business leader is by taking the time to be with yourself.

- Step away from your comfort zone by setting monthly goals and pushing the limits through extra activities, environments, or exposures.

- When you get out of your comfort zone, there are no shortcuts or detours; there is only work, grit, and tenacity to achieve your dreams.

Chapter 3:

The Power of Growth Mindset

"There is nothing either 'good or bad,' but 'thinking' makes it so. It is the "perception" that makes things what they are. Good and bad are in our minds. Our mindset and mental attitude determine how we will interpret and respond to situations." ~ **Erik Pevernagie**

Early in Michael Jordan's basketball career, he faced many hurdles. Michael Jordan was born in Brooklyn, New York. Still, he spent his childhood in a rural house in Wilmington, North Carolina, surrounded by generations of family dating back to his great-grandfather. James Jordan, Michael's father, was a maintenance worker who later became a supervisor at General Electric; he introduced Jordan to his first athletic love, baseball, but built a basketball court in his backyard. That backyard court was the canvas for Jordan to develop his basketball genius, playing his brother Larry one-on-one, unleashing the beast of his competitive spirit. The two went full steam at each other on the court every day until bedtime, with their mother, Deloris, stepping in to end the fights when things got too heated.

However, even with his growing basketball skills, the high school varsity basketball team cut Jordan, which was heartbreaking. But rather than giving up, Michael used the setback to fuel his determination to improve, leading to his meteoric rise in the sport. In his career, Michael was no stranger to intense competition from other skilled players and formidable teams.

The pressure to perform at an elite level and outshine his opponents was a constant struggle, but his intense mindset motivated him to elevate his game. Even after Michael's dad passed in 1993, and suffering a devastating broken foot that put him in rehab for months, Michael's mindset and mental fortitude allowed him to overcome and become one of the greatest basketball players of our time. He never wavered and overcame continuously.

Despite these struggles, Michael Jordan's resilience, determination, and unwavering belief in his ability to overcome adversity define his legacy and are a testament to the power of perseverance, resilience, and a growth-oriented mindset in achieving exceptional success. His willingness to face challenges, learn from failures, and strive for improvement embodies the essence of embracing growth on the path to happiness and fulfillment.

When my wife and I started Marigold Academy, it didn't take long for us to realize we had much to learn and had to tackle it all head-on. The realization hit us that we needed to exhibit strength of mind and be perfectly aligned, recognizing that a weak or timid approach would not suffice. Instead, our efforts had to be one hundred percent dedicated to the cause. Today, if someone were to ask what word could describe our dedication to developing our robust curriculum and nurturing environment for our children and staff, it would be relentless, followed by having a solid mindset. From the beginning, we had a focused mindset on directing the curriculum, which enabled us to pursue our newfound passion for childcare and developing children's lives. I wake up daily with the mindset of growth, making Marigold Academy a better place for our children, teachers, parents, and franchisees.

A mindset is the set of attitudes and beliefs that shape how an individual interprets different situations, relationships, and abilities. Mindset represents the underlying mental frame through which a person filters information, forms judgments, and determines corresponding actions and responses.

Mindsets are often subconscious assumptions we make about life and our abilities. These preconceived notions stay fixed unless the individual gains awareness of potential blind spots and shifts their mindset. Different mindsets hold the potential to either limit someone or help them succeed. Mindsets affect what a person thinks they can do or cannot do. As a leader, when you envision what you want to achieve and are unwilling to settle, you tap into an inner reserve of strength. With a mindset focused on growth, you can surround yourself with positive energy that motivates you on tough days and a firm commitment that guarantees gradual progress. What others said you were incapable of becomes possible. Outstanding achievements take time, grit, an almost stubborn refusal to give up, and a relentless belief in the power of everyday hard work.

According to psychologist Carol Dweck, having a growth mindset means viewing challenges as exciting rather than intimidating. So rather than thinking, "Oh, I'm going to reveal my weaknesses," you say, "Wow, here's a chance to grow." When you view setbacks as opportunities for growth rather than failures, you are more likely to bounce back and become a more decisive leader.

The secret to success is having a mindset that embraces growth, which involves being willing to face challenges and learn from failures. But with all this talk, what does a mindset mean? Dr. Carol Dweck states, "Mindset is a belief that you have about yourself and your most basic qualities." It's the story you tell yourself about who you are, and it shapes your thoughts, feelings, and actions. The right mindset is crucial for success in any area of life and is the difference between success and failure. Believing in strengthening your abilities through hard work and dedication is the key to unlocking your full potential.

While working at Yazaki North America as an engineer, I faced challenges that tested my mindset and fortitude. There, I realized my genuine passion and core strengths were in financial management and operations. However, with my background and experience in engineering, I didn't have the proper skills or knowledge needed to be in the world of finance. Instead of stopping there and staying where I was, I pursued an MBA to learn core finance, accounting, and financial risk management competencies as I continued working full-time as an engineer. While pursuing my MBA in finance from Michigan State University, I risked it all following my inner tingling and mindset for higher growth.

I left my well-paid full-time engineering job and accepted an unpaid internship for an asset management firm in Michigan to gain the skills and experience to excel in the field. What made this move even riskier was that I was told upfront that this internship would not lead to a full-time job at the firm. On the surface, it was a step back, but it was a monumental step forward, helping me gain proficiency in those areas to pursue a new career. Many discouraged me from making this move during the housing and financial meltdown of 2008. All I knew was to follow what was inside me, knowing it would break new ground into a new career and opportunity. That chance I took by following my inner instinct opened doors for me in financial services, and I landed my first six-figure job upon finishing my MBA later that year.

This gave me the confidence to jump when it felt right in my gut and not fear the outcome. That incident gave me the courage and confidence to take on many more serendipitous challenges later in my life, including entering the childcare industry. Through it all, I gained the much-needed confidence to franchise my business, which I knew nothing about except having a dream and a vision of what it could become.

As a leader and new franchisee, understanding your mindset is essential and means seeing challenges as opportunities for personal development and gaining knowledge. As you mature, you build resilience in the face of setbacks, using them as steppingstones for future success, seeking feedback and constructive criticism to improve yourself and your business.

You can learn anything if you believe in your ability to learn and grow. However, if you believe that your abilities are fixed, you may find yourself stuck and often making excuses for not acting. Procrastination is based on fear of failure. When you fear failure, you avoid challenges that may show shortcomings. This is human nature, but limiting yourself with a fixed mindset can cripple your progress, stopping you from taking risks and restricting your growth opportunities.

However, promoting a growth mindset empowers you to overcome obstacles confidently as a leader and individual, promoting learning and resilience. With a mindset that embraces growth, you can always improve and reach your goals. Renowned author Stephen Covey once remarked, "Your attitude determines your altitude." Indeed. Suppose you root your attitude in a fixed mindset, believing that your abilities are predetermined and unchangeable. In that case, it can lead to stagnation and procrastination, a fear of failure, and it kills your willingness to take risks or pursue challenges.

As a leader and franchise business owner, your mindset shapes your actions and your perseverance and outcomes. Psychologist Dr. Angela Duckworth, said, "Grit is passion and perseverance for long-term goals. Grit is having stamina. Grit is sticking with your future, day in and day out." We all face challenges, and often, many of them seem overwhelming and even impossible. However, if you change your mindset and embrace growth, you will build momentum by tackling challenges and gaining confidence in your ability to overcome them.

Having a fixed mindset can hinder success, unlike having a growth mindset. Dr. Dweck stated, "The view you adopt for yourself profoundly affects how you lead your life." As a new franchisee, you will face challenges. Still, by putting effort into developing your mindset, you can build resilience and learn to view setbacks as temporary hurdles you can overcome. As you face the storms, you can emerge more assertive on the other side.

From what I've learned, developing a growth mindset is similar to playing an engaging and rewarding video game. For instance, imagine a multiplayer game where players navigate a universe of challenges, quests, and mysteries. To win this game, having a mindset that focuses on personal growth is important. Players with a growth mindset view each new level as an opportunity to succeed and come out on top by learning, adjusting, and getting better.

The same is true in Marigold Academy—franchising and running your business. You must approach the business's progress through failures and setbacks and unlock it with the mindset that you will learn the moves to win the game. With each new level unlocked, you gain self-efficacy to fuel motivation as you grow with a positive mindset.

You will unlock higher levels of achievement and gain new abilities, approaches, and techniques to succeed. Our progress shows that nothing, not even ourselves, remains fixed forever. Progress changes how we perceive what was once difficult and unattainable, making it a matter of mindset and opening doors to new opportunities, adventures, and risk-taking.

Many renowned individuals show a great eagerness to learn and develop, never allowing setbacks or obstacles to hinder their drive and success. One example of this is Albert Einstein, who is recognized as one of the most famous scientists and inventors ever. Why? Through his achievements and failures, he is a prime example of having a strong mindset, as he experienced more failure than most in his lifetime. Einstein said, "I have not failed. I've found 10,000 ways that won't work." As an inspiration to us all, he kept trying to change the world through his mindset and strong initiative, and you can, too.

And who could forget the Harry Potter books by author J. K. Rowling? The billionaire Harry Potter author was a struggling single mom on welfare when she began writing her first book in cafes. Planning the Harry Potter books, every publisher rejected her. Often, she waited weeks and even months to receive a rejection letter. Things got so bad that she waited over six months to see if a publisher would even consider publishing her book. Despite the heartbreaking rejections, she believed in herself and the Harry Potter story, finding a publisher, finishing what she started.

Even Colonel Sanders, the founder of KFC, was a man who had a clear vision for the company, achieving his dreams with hard work and facing the challenges that came his way. Sanders said, "The more I failed, the more I learned."

Along the journey of building and franchising Marigold Academy, I have developed specific strategies to face the challenges in leadership and franchising. Let's examine:

Aim to Learn, Not Just Pass Tests.

Make learning your primary aim in all your endeavors, rather than just trying to pass tests. Emphasize developing fundamental abilities rather than fixating on marks. Authentic learning and understanding involve a genuine concern for the process, not just the outcome.

Changing Negative Self-Talk.

To learn and improve, change your mindset to view problems and setbacks as learning opportunities to improve. Switch your thinking by saying to yourself, "I haven't mastered this yet," versus "I failed and can't do this." Movie star and Karate expert Bruce Lee said, "Don't speak negatively about yourself, even as a joke. Your body doesn't know the difference. Words are energy, and they cast spells; that's why it's called spelling. Change how you speak about yourself, and you can change your life."

It's hard to avoid negative talk about ourselves. It is human nature for us to get down about what we can't do or lack the ability to accomplish. To beat this internal dialogue, do your best to think positively, decreasing negative self-talk for the long term. Our brains naturally focus on the negative, especially if someone tells us we're doing fantastic but note one issue we must work on. We naturally focus on the negative; often, one negative statement can ruin our mood.

However, dwelling on the negative can harm our success in the modern world, so we must teach our minds to think optimistically. What does thinking positively entail? Thinking positively means adopting a more optimistic outlook on life. It is choosing to focus on the positive over the negative and keeping optimistic.

Over time, this new mindset will become everyday thinking. It will take time and conscious effort; and may take a while to grasp, but you can vastly improve your well-being if you catch and reframe self-limiting thoughts. When thinking negatively, train your brain to ask a trigger sentence. Say to yourself, "Is that how I want to talk to myself? Is this healthy?" Train your mind to ask those questions to help you reset and think better thoughts. Be your personal encouragement coach. Hold yourself accountable. If you can't seem to get a grip on this approach, there isn't anything wrong with getting a real coach or the right mentor who will help you see things from different perspectives.

Get Help from a Mentor Coach.

One of the main reasons I am where I am today is because of the help and guidance of mentors and coaches along the way. I surround myself with experienced business coaches and mentors because I believe having a mentor who has gone before you and paved the way is essential to a successful life and growing a successful business. Bestselling Author Daniel H. Pink once said, "I'm so high on coaching because it supports expanding your perspective. And the wider your perspective, the more effective you can be, because you have more vantage points to evaluate from."

***

Vignette: Personal Note from Kruti Shah

Jay believes in mentors, talking and learning from people who have walked the walk before him. He never missed a meeting when he hired his business coach because he learned the most from others who inspired and empowered him to be the best leader.

***

Throughout my professional career, I've had several mentors who have helped shape who I am today. They all had unique strengths and characteristics. Having them as mentors taught me many skills that I now use as a leader.

One prominent and influential mentor I had was Michael O'Neill, CEO of Preferred Sands, a hydraulic fracking enterprise. He saw my great potential and took me under his wing to teach me the ropes. Under his direction, I learned to take prudent risks and how to leverage my potential in analytical skills to identify alternative and efficient ways to improve our supply chain, lower expenses, and increase margins on products we sold.

Being detail-oriented, Michael showed me how to work with private equity firms and investment banks to raise funding for future expansion. As a leader, he was aware of high-performing staff and quickly eliminated underperformers. In his world, he wanted to surround himself with high-performing employees with opportunities and assignments to push them beyond their capabilities. Through his guidance as a leader, he was a courageous man who taught me much of what I know now, which has helped me become an influential business leader.

As a new franchisee and business leader, with a mentor or coach, you can discuss your areas of concern and challenges without worrying about judgment and objectively evaluate your ideas and progress. Most entrepreneurs are often deeply involved in their day-to-day operations, which many times hinders their ability to have a big-picture perspective.

Looking inward, with the guidance of a mentor, can help identify blind spots and unforeseen areas of opportunity. Ruth Bader Ginsburg said, "A mentor allows you to learn more about yourself than you ever thought possible. They help you see your strengths and weaknesses to make informed decisions."

A mentor's regular input keeps you on track in pursuing goals by holding you accountable toward meeting milestones. Regular check-ins do this, ensuring you execute verbal commitments and encouraging you to keep pushing your limits. Using a mentor, you can tap into their experience of what they have gone through to learn how to maneuver through those challenges. Like playing a video game, you learn patterns and pathways to use and others to avoid. By drawing on their experiences to avoid common (and sometimes costly) mistakes, you can prevent predictable issues you fear.

When I decided to franchise Marigold Academy, I was unfamiliar with the world of franchising. Becoming a franchisor comes with distinct challenges: from running thriving childcare centers to helping others achieve their entrepreneurial dreams, all while guiding them to follow our proven system, and adapting to our culture and processes to be successful. This was all new to me, and realizing that, I reached out to coaches and mentors in the world of franchising to guide me with this new profound journey I was about to embark on.

I consulted with franchising experts Gary Occhiogrosso, Alicia Miller, and Steven Beagelman to assist me with this journey. They have a lot of experience helping new brands succeed by following proven methods and avoiding common obstacles. Without their mentoring, I would not be where I am today as a franchisor. Their wealth of knowledge and wisdom has given me the tools and techniques to navigate the complex world of franchising.

Vignette: Personal Note from Gary Occhiogrosso

Jay came to me through Steven, who I know and trusted to vet all true professionals. From day one, Jay Shah had that special leadership mentality that drives and never stops pursuing knowledge in the name of helping everyone around him. Jay cares about his staff, teachers, families, community, and most of all, his business and family. He is strong-minded, willed, and stops at nothing to ensure he leaves a long-lasting legacy with Marigold Academy.

Don't Be Afraid of Criticism.

With a positive mindset, you gain strength in overcoming criticism. Taking criticism as a lesson becomes a way to learn what went wrong. Use any criticism to your advantage by turning it into feedback and seeking takeaways you can implement instead of letting the criticism make you feel attacked. It's all about mindset in those situations and how you look at them.

Take Risks Without Fearing Failure.

To overcome fear and embrace failure, it is crucial to cultivate a mindset that thrives on growth. When things don't work out, failure teaches you what you need to improve and avoid doing. Motivational expert and author Sanjeev Himachali, said, "Criticism is part of learning and growth. This means you are learning something new and growing from your current state. If you are not getting criticized, you are not taking enough risk to learn something new and grow." In anything you do, changing your thinking to know the goal isn't a perfect performance. Instead, it's about learning and improving what you can do better.

Celebrate the Journey Over Destination

Celebrate the journey over the destination as you grow in a positive framework and a healthy mindset. Acknowledge smaller milestones of improvement, not just the end achievement. And along the way, never forget your family and loved ones. They are your support system, the backbone of who you are. Your family and circles are why you've become the leader you want to be. Your family and loved ones count, so while you're building your new franchise and improving your inner self, don't forget to 'live' while chasing your dreams.

***

Important Points

- Mindsets are the often subconscious assumptions we make about life and our abilities.

- As a leader and new franchisee, understanding your mindset is essential for personal growth and development.

- A growth mindset means seeing challenges as opportunities to develop and gain knowledge, take risks, and not fear failing.

- Get an experienced coach to help you navigate your struggles and shortcomings to elevate and achieve peak performance.

- Taking criticism becomes a way to learn what went wrong as a lesson.

- Life is a journey, not a destination. Take care of those around you and your loved ones.

Chapter 4:

Get Clarity on What's Next?

"The best way to succeed is to have a specific Intent, a clear Vision, a plan of Action, and the ability to maintain Clarity. Those are the Four Pillars of Success. It never fails!" ~ **Steve Maraboli, *Life, the Truth, and Being Free.***

Mohandas Karamchand Gandhi was born on October 2, 1869, in Porbandar, a tiny city in Gujarat, India. From an early age, stories of valor and bravery attracted him and motivated him to leave his mark on the world. His fights for freedom, justice, and equality exhibited dedication that few have matched. His narrative of accomplishment teaches us that no matter how daunting the odds appear, we can overcome them with effort, devotion, willpower, and genuine clarity and direction.

After being sent to London to study law, Gandhi returned to India and started practicing law, getting involved in the Indian National Congress. Gandhi believed India could achieve independence through peaceful civil disobedience. He advocated nonviolence, as seen by his renowned Salt March in 1930. This march denounced the British salt tariff and began the Indian independence movement.

With his clarity, direction, and intelligence, Gandhi's leadership brought attention to the battle for Indian independence and encouraged people across the country to fight for their rights. Gandhi's leadership abilities and dedication earned him a devoted following in India and worldwide. He received the Nobel Peace Prize in 1948 for promoting peace and nonviolence. His legacy continues to be remembered today as a sign of persistence and fortitude. He showed how even one person, with true clarity and direction, can make a difference and effect positive change in the world.

When we entered the childcare industry in 2019, our Bloomfield center was thriving. It was operating at full capacity and exhibited happy children, teachers, and parents. Other schools modeled our culture and philosophy, and everything was going well for us until the COVID-19 pandemic hit us in 2020, shutting the country down in lockdown and bringing us to a complete stop.

Our center thrived with its nurturing, high-quality childcare environment, but the shutdown blindsided us. We had borrowed a lot of money to operate the business, and less than a year later, we were facing financial ruin and closure, with zero income. Everything was up in the air and scary, and I spent many sleepless nights trying to figure out a direction and what to do.

Through it all, I never gave up. Eventually, they lifted the state-mandated shutdown, allowing us to reopen. However, many parents and teachers didn't return to school because of health concerns. But I had a clear objective, and I stuck to our vision. By believing in our mission, we adapted and established a clear focus on creating a healthy, safe, best-care, and nurturing environment for all our children and staff.

Through the protocols and guidelines for the pandemic, we improved our health and safety procedures with genuine clarity and direction. We gained momentum by investing in enhanced cleaning procedures and following safety guidelines from health officials and leaders. It all paid off, as parents in our community took notice of our commitment. Parents and teachers started returning to our center, trusting our commitment to ensuring health and cleanliness through proactive measures.

But it took a year of hard work to make things good again, and the only way we did it was to stay clear on our initial goals and vision. Without a clear mission and foundational principles, this would not have been achievable for our childcare business.

Our experience through COVID-19 taught us that running and growing a childcare center is more than just providing a service; it's about building trust and emotional connections with parents, staff, and the community. By delivering exceptional care in a safe, nurturing environment, we fostered the confidence and peace of mind that parents needed to entrust us with their most precious gifts: their children. This clarity and focus on our unwavering commitment to quality and compassion is establishing our long-term sustainability and success.

Clarity is the cornerstone of effective leadership, enabling successful organizations and franchises to thrive. However, what does clarity mean, and what makes it significant? Clarity in business is conveying ideas, goals, and expectations to others and us. Clarity forms the basis for developing strategies and initiatives in business and leadership. But what criteria can evaluate clarity and your leadership effectiveness?

Judging leadership success isn't just about profits. It's about building capabilities and a corporate culture that can make progress in the long run. Here are a few things we look at when evaluating leadership effectiveness:

- **Strategic Vision:** Setting direction, rallying support, making effective plans.

- **Results Delivery:** Achieving key goals, Key Performance Indicators (KPIs), and business outcomes.

- **Team Development:** Build skilled, motivated teams and grow talent.

- **Culture and Values:** Inspiring shared values and peak performance.

- **Communication:** Explain clearly, listen, and bring people together.

- **Decision Making:** Showing sound judgment and problem-solving daily and during crises.

- **Emotional Intelligence:** Demonstrating self-awareness, empathy, and composure.

Not having a clear understanding of your leadership styles and goals is one of the main reasons businesses fail. A *Harvard Business Review* study revealed that this lack of clarity kills many businesses. Companies with clear and concise goals are twice as likely to achieve than as those without.

Leaders need clarity to communicate, make decisions, and execute tasks, which aids in defining their effectiveness as leaders. Leadership expert John C. Maxwell said, "Clarity serves as a counterbalance to chaos." Without clear direction, things can spiral out of control, leaving you feeling lost. You cannot achieve authentic leadership when you appear lost without proper direction. There must be objectives and goals; confusion and demotivation can undermine your goals and vision, leading to failure.

Perhaps you're wondering about the strategies for setting clear goals and objectives. Let's look at some ways and their advantages:

- **Connect to a Higher Purpose**: Tie your goals to the big picture—the company vision and mission. Then, goals feel more meaningful than everyday tasks and help reach dreams. Provide direction and rally teams behind a united purpose rather than disjointed activities and diluting force. Explaining the big "WHY" behind work helps teams come together under one mission.

- **Visualize the End State:** Imagine goals already met and visualize the team celebrating after the hard work and the job well done. Take the task with the end game in mind and work backward to determine what you need to make it real later.
- **Co-Construct Them:** Work together on goals, including context, ensuring agreement from the team doing the work. They will care more than if bosses assign targets.

What is the secret superpower to achieving genuine clarity now that we have this? Start by allowing yourself space to achieve consistent growth and authentic clarity. Getting away and thinking without distraction is the best place to be. Monitor and discipline yourself to eliminate lost time and crucial attention caused by mindless scrolling on social media and other distractions. To gain clarity, you must make time every day to "be." Clear your mind of mental distractions to establish a connection with your authentic self and greater purpose. Take some time each day to be present with yourself. Focus your attention. Reflect deeply. Take deep breaths with purpose. This is where it all starts.

Seeking awareness of your values provides personal space, healing benefits, and clarity. When considering your career and business goals, ask yourself: "What matters most to me, and why?"

My wife and I took the time to write what was most important to us when building a legacy for our children and establishing a long-lasting entrepreneurial journey. We cared about the most important attributes that parents, the community, children, and staff would gain by being part of Marigold Academy through our clear mission and vision. This strategic move established our principles and company values. In the words of Brené Brown, a New York Times bestselling author and renowned professor, "Our values serve as a compass for navigating life. We can't figure out who we are unless we know what our values are."

Discovering your true self and passions is crucial for clarity. What are your passions? What aspirations do you have? Knowing your passions is essential to unlocking your peak performance potential. I found that posing these questions helped me achieve clarity as a leader.

- The thing I am most enthusiastic about is:
- When I am happiest is:
- I am my best self when:
- What gives me the most energy is:

Knowing your purpose also results in clarity. While purpose was a topic of discussion in prior chapters, it is vital to recognize your challenges and areas of discomfort to better comprehend your future actions. Give thought to:

- What makes you feel the most satisfied and content?
- What is the purpose of your mission?
- Who is the person you aspire to be?
- How do I wish to be perceived by others?
- What is the impact I want to leave on people and the world?

You need to summarize the answers and craft a mission statement that you can convey in an elevator pitch. Allocate time for this. Put your words into writing. Gain further understanding through introspection by posing the question, "Where do you envision yourself in five years?"

Merge your insights from earlier steps to form a strong mental image of your aspirations in five years.

Imagine your life as a story, and you are the author of the next chapter. What do you hope to achieve in your personal and professional life? In what way have you made a difference?

The company's staff usually has high confidence in its leaders, underscoring the need for clear communication from executives about the team's ability to perform tasks, adapt, and exceed expectations. When you define your role and responsibilities as a leader and align them with the organization's objectives, mission, and goals, it promotes teamwork. Marigold Academy, companywide, works to encourage a team atmosphere and work environment.

Empowering your team has the potential to boost performance. Leaders receptive to new ideas and opinions from their team members experience increased empowerment and improved job performance.

As a community leader, I've learned that when leaders care about their staff's long-term growth, it motivates them to perform at their best.

Marigold Academy Franchise offers our exceptional staff the chance to grow into corporate leadership roles. The ability to advance in one's career empowers individuals to create legacies and embark on remarkable professional journeys. Training new franchise owners has the power to create many legacies for students and staff, affecting classrooms nationwide. We offer opportunities for community members, professionals, and ambitious entrepreneurs who want to start their own small businesses, with a focus on clarity.

Marigold Academy and my corporate background have influenced me to give back. I take pleasure in assisting skilled individuals in establishing their personal legacies via franchised Marigold Academy childcare centers. Every morning, this mission energizes me by empowering teachers and entrepreneurs to pursue their purpose and create growth opportunities. Marigold Academy came into being because of its strong mission and vision, emphasizing community empowerment and personal legacies.

I foster unity among our staff by promoting clear communication and shared vision. By doing this, everyone gains awareness of what matters and can collaborate. Our shared goals unite us, whether it's achieving KPIs, enhancing our curriculum and processes, or expanding into new areas. Knowing that what I leave behind as a leader and franchisor is part of my legacy is a source of pride for me.

A recent Gallup survey shows that a mere 13% of employees worldwide feel their bosses are effective communicators. When communication is unclear, it can negatively affect employee engagement and the overall success of the organization. The absence of clear goals from management results in a lack of motivation and accomplishment from the staff.

McKinsey & Company discovered that valuing transparency in decision-making increases a company's likelihood of success by four times. By sharing strategic decisions, leaders enable their staff to align goals and make informed choices for the organization.

When business dealings lack clarity, it can cause misunderstandings, conflicts, and missed opportunities. For example, the Project Management Institute's survey attributed 56% of project failures to poor communication. This emphasizes how clarity, or its absence, can affect the outcome of a project or initiative.

Warren Bennis defined leadership as, "The ability to transform vision into reality." The translation process relies on leaders communicating a clear vision to their teams. Leaders who communicate an inspiring future vision, establish definite goals, and maintain open lines of communication with their teams are more likely to foster trust and loyalty.

During my tenure at Yazaki North America (YNA) as an engineer, I came across a unique process called Japanese Kanban. While first designed for manufacturing, I've discovered that the core principles of the Kanban process apply to any business and effective leadership. Kanban, a Japanese production system, employs visual cues to implement "lean principles" and lower manufacturing expenses. In the 1940s, Toyota Production System implemented Kanban for inventory management, faster time to market, and improved quality. Kanban continues to be a well-hidden gem for improving quality and clarity in work, and individuals can apply it in both business and personal contexts.

To provide clarity on Marigold Academy's operations and process, I further adopted the Kanban workflow management approach using specific guidelines:

1. Limit the amount of work happening at each step. Finish existing work before adding new ones.

2. Review progress daily in team meetings to address what is stuck or not working.

3. Follow processes to uphold transparency. Hold each team member other accountable.

4. Improve by finding minor fixes to issues.

The key focus is on delivering value seamlessly and minimizing waste. Kanban uses visual representation to identify problems and ensures a balance between speed and workload by clarifying corrective methods and processes to everyone. Using data, teams can work towards bigger goals by making incremental improvements.

Our franchise has implemented specific steps and processes to enhance the Kanban process. Clarity is crucial, so franchisees must trust the process, follow it, and avoid taking shortcuts by focusing on one task at a time. It carries special importance. With Marigold Academy, we have crafted our franchise intake system to ensure it is uncomplicated and replicable. Our established procedures follow the principles of Kanban.

- **Exploratory Call:** Introductory call and get to know each other.

- **Disclosure and Confidentiality**: Receive our Franchise Disclosure Document (FDD) to learn more about our business.

- **Executive Call:** Meet Jay and Kruti Shah, founding members of Marigold Academy.

- **Discovery Day:** Franchisee visits our schools in person, exposing the new owner to the childcare environment and what it's like to own and operate a childcare center.

- **Contracts:** Contracts and Legal Process begins in drafting agreements.

- **Location:** Find a location with the help of our Real Estate team.

- **Site Design:** Design and construction of the site under Marigold standards.

- **Back-end Operations:** Marketing, hiring, and training leading up to your school's grand opening and launch.

Marigold Academy recognizes demonstrating consistent exceptional care and education. No matter which location you choose, you can count on the same high standards and a smooth experience. Our schools follow a standardized approach for everything, including daily routines, drop-off/pickup procedures, hiring practices, and staff training.

The curriculum at Marigold Academy is designed by our expert team to provide a consistent and top-notch education for every child, regardless of the center they attend. Our team of experts has developed a comprehensive program, covering daily and monthly learning objectives to support children's growth and development.

Our team has worked to streamline our operations for a seamless process for our owners, operators, and teachers. We have removed uncertainty and enabled our staff to concentrate on what is important—delivering nurturing care and engaging learning experiences to our students—through establishing proven systems and procedures. By building our vendor relationships, we guarantee that every Marigold Academy has access to the best resources and supplies. We have partnered with reliable providers who are committed to excellence.

We attribute our success at Marigold Academy to our proven protocols and unwavering commitment to consistency. By implementing these established practices, we can assure our stakeholders of the high-quality care and education we offer to every child. Adhering to the process and maintaining consistency are key aspects of strong leadership in franchising.

A one-size-fits-all mindset cannot apply to leadership. There are multiple leadership philosophies, each having their own strengths and weaknesses. Autocratic leadership is all about centralized control and top-down decision-making. This style is all about getting orders from the top. Yes, it works, but it can make your team feel disconnected and create a stuffy vibe among the staff.

An organized approach to leadership involves democratic style, where the team reaches decisions through group consensus. While it can empower team members, as a leader, you risk slowing down the process because of the time required for consensus building.

Another effective approach to inspire teams towards a shared vision is transformational leadership. Transformational leaders rally teams by embodying the change they seek. Their contagious passion for a bold vision of the future inspires others to believe in and work towards making it a reality. You might be familiar with some people who have already applied transformational leadership.

Take, for example, the renowned NBA All-Star coach Phil Jackson and his Zen philosophy. Jackson became one of the greatest coaches because of his adoption of a coaching style inspired by the transformational leadership of another. His coaching style prioritized teamwork, effective management of star players and their egos, and fostering open communication, embodying a transformational approach.

As leaders at Marigold Academy, we strive to bring about transformation. Our company takes pride in motivating teams and staff by communicating our vision. Franchising and leadership share similarities. When the team's goals and expectations align, it enhances collaboration. The dynamic nature of clarity in business and leadership propels successful organizations, effective leadership, and overall team engagement. According to Richard Branson, a prominent business magnate, effective communication is the most crucial skill a leader can have. Returning to the main point, effective communication starts with clarity—the skill to express ideas, objectives, and expectations and comprehensibly.

In today's cutthroat business world, leaders must possess exceptional communication skills, decision-making abilities, and strategic planning expertise. How does clarity contribute to achieving success? There are several ways:

- Setting clear goals and KPIs. These are a set of measurable values that businesses use to evaluate their performance and progress toward their goals. For clarity in business, KPIs measure communication and collaboration among team members, customer satisfaction, and overall business effectiveness.

- Clarity focused on the most important priorities keeps daily work on track. Teams don't get sidetracked by small stuff.
- When direction seems unclear, misguided work by staff can waste resources and time.
- If leaders cannot convey a simple strategy, teams feel uncertain about what decisions should get top priority.
- Identifying and communicating the company's purpose and values attracts the right people. They will care about the culture and leaders' vision.

By promoting a culture of effective communication, organizations can boost employee engagement, foster innovation, and attain sustained success in a competitive market. As the famous American author H. Jackson Browne Jr. stated, "The illusion of successful communication is the greatest obstacle." Be careful not to get trapped in this situation. Make clarity a top priority in your business and leadership practices to ensure your organization thrives amidst uncertainty and change.

***

Important Points

- Clear communication is the key to working together, forming partnerships, and negotiating well. When everyone on the team knows the goals and expectations, they will collaborate better to achieve them.
- Successful organizations and franchises thrive on clarity, which forms the foundation for effective leadership.

- Clarity is the state of being transparent and the quality of being intelligible.
- Clearly define what style of leadership you resonate with. Focus on your strengths.
- It is the ability to communicate ideas, goals, and expectations in a way easily understood by others and us.

Phase II: Commitment

Chapter 5:

Failure to Feedback

"It's not whether you get knocked down, it's whether you get back up." ~ **Vince Lombardi**

There isn't anyone on the planet who hasn't seen or heard of a Ford automobile. However, many are unaware that Henry Ford, the car's owner and inventor, transformed his failures, mistakes, and tragedies into opportunities for new beginnings. Ford transformed his failure into a steppingstone towards success.

Born in 1863, Ford began his journey as an aspiring inventor and business owner at a young age. In school, even as a small boy, he showed a strong interest in mechanical things and learned all he could about engineering. At twelve, Ford started a small machine shop, and by the time he reached fifteen, he created a steam engine. In this moment of clarity, Ford followed his passion with his technical skills. Soon Ford left his home to work as an apprentice in different automotive companies to develop his knowledge and skills.

Taking his knowledge and skills to the next level, Ford used his experiments in building a self-propelled vehicle, which was the catalyst and the beginning of the Ford engines. Continuing his efforts, following his vision, Ford designed another engine with a new mechanism that was mounted on a frame. That frame became the first automobile, and in 1899, he founded the Detroit Automobile Company, which he later renamed the Henry Ford Company.

This was the beginning of what seemed to be Ford's end. Everything unraveled, and many problems emerged as he started manufacturing. Soon, the company experienced the sting of high costs for equipment, workers, and many other things, and the financial outlook was so bleak that it forced Ford to leave the company.

However, Ford and his career did not stop. He kept going, learning from his mistakes, and he rose from the ashes, starting the current Ford Motor Company. Ford's problem was that many people, right after the depression, couldn't afford an expensive car. Ford saw a niche and changed the game by making automobiles more affordable for the everyday man. This was the game changer.

Once he dropped the price from $850 to $290 for the company's most popular car, the Model T, the company had difficulty fulfilling all the orders. To answer the demand, Ford continued his vision by mass-producing vehicles in large plants; and the Ford Motor Company began to thrive and dominate the market. Even though Ford passed away decades ago, his achievements have left a lasting legacy in the industry. Ford is the ideal illustration of pursuing your goals despite setbacks and learning from failures.

While there are countless stories of people pursuing their dreams, how often do we come across tales of triumph over adversity through learning from major failures? Only a few. Both our country's leaders and ordinary business fighters have stories that illustrate how they used their failures to achieve their dreams. Failure is not a myth; it can lead to success.

There's an adage that states, "Feedback is a gift." But what does that mean? Feedback is essential for growth and improvement in business. It's the process through which companies and individuals gain knowledge, adjust, and generate new ideas. Regrettably, companies and individuals often overlook or mishandle feedback, resulting in the cycle known as "failure to feedback."

Feedback is vital for the growth and success of teams and staff in the workplace and any other organization. In running and managing a Marigold Academy franchise, it is crucial to embrace the "feedback concept" by offering and receiving constructive criticism to enhance the work of both individuals and your staff. Without input, it's challenging to pinpoint problem areas and develop strategies to tackle them.

In Marigold Academy's business model, we provide several ways for people to give feedback as a loop: anonymous questionnaires, peer-to-peer feedback sessions, and regular performance reviews are just a few. In addition, among other feedback channels, we have used our social media platforms, online forums, and client testimonials to guide our operations. By welcoming comments, individuals and organizations can foster a culture of development and ongoing improvement.

The Failure-to-Feedback Cycle, also known as the Failure Feedback Loop, is a continuous process that allows individuals and groups to learn from mistakes and enhance future success. This loop begins with a failure or setback, prompting reflection and analysis to identify the underlying causes. Through this introspection, I've gained significant lessons and insights that will guide my response to similar situations in the future.

The Failure to Feedback Cycle highlights the value of accepting failure as an inevitable component of learning and development rather than attempting to avoid or minimize it. Teams and organizations may cultivate a culture of continuous innovation and improvement by taking part in this cycle of failure, reflection, learning, and application, leading to long-term success and growth.

Importance of Constructive Feedback in Business.

Business success and growth rely on receiving constructive feedback. As a leader, you can assist staff members in recognizing growth opportunities by providing them with specific and practical feedback on their performance. Giving constructive criticism builds trust and open communication and creates a positive workplace environment. When you, as a leader, have encouraging talks with your teams, it boosts morale and productivity. Open communication helps gather vital information about the organization's pros and cons, allowing you to make wise decisions and support ongoing development.

Regular feedback boosts staff engagement and commitment to company goals. This has the potential to increase job satisfaction, productivity, and loyalty.

What Are the Issues a Franchise Would Face When There is a Lack of Open Communication?

Ineffective communication can have a detrimental impact on the growth and success of a franchise brand. A major challenge arises from the differing priorities and goals of the franchisor and franchisees. If we fail to communicate clearly, franchisees may misunderstand our goals and compromise our tactics, which could have a negative impact on the brand.

Another big issue that can happen when communication is lacking is that problem-solving doesn't work. Franchisees might struggle to fix issues if they don't think their concerns are being heard or taken seriously. This can cause problems that impact how happy customers are and how well things go.

Not having good communication between franchisees and the franchisor, and within the franchisee community, can disrupt trust, teamwork, the work vibe, and decision-making. It could make it more difficult for the franchise to adjust to shifting consumer demands and market conditions.

When we don't have open communication, our brand standards suffer, and we lose out on opportunities to innovate. Franchise owners might struggle to get the brand rules or see how sharing ideas with the total business can be beneficial.

Importance of Honest Dialogue Across the Company.

A healthy work environment requires open communication and honest dialogue between management and staff. Fostering trust and open communication cultivates a positive workplace culture. As a leader, ensure you support and promote open dialogue with your teams, teachers, and staff.

Avoiding Fear with Your Teams.

The fear of reprisal is a significant hurdle. If staff members are fearful of negative repercussions, such as a lack of promotion, undesirable tasks, or potential dismissal, they may be reluctant to voice their opinions or offer honest feedback. Fear stems from a lack of trust in leaders or a company culture that does not place importance on open communication.

In any organization, there is a hierarchy, and often, that comes with a power dynamic within the organization. This might make staff anxious about speaking to higher-ups because they fear that their comments will be ignored or seen as challenging authority.

Communication styles and personalities may sometimes get in the way of having genuine conversations. When individuals feel uneasy about giving or receiving feedback, misunderstandings and arguments can hinder open communication.

Lack of time and poor communication can also hinder honest conversations. When work gets busy, staff members might feel pressured to prioritize tasks instead of having meaningful discussions.

How Can You Get Your Team to Not Fear Negative Consequences?

In their book *Feedback: The Last Best Hope for Success at Work and Success in Life,* Douglas Stone and Sheila Heen said, "It's hard to hear feedback, and there's often misunderstanding between a feedback-giver and a feedback-receiver: When a person receives feedback, she feels it's unfair or untrue. But when she gives feedback, she feels the other person isn't listening or understanding it. Organizations and self-help books often focus on teaching how to give feedback better to reconcile this disconnect. The key, though, is learning how to receive it better. After all, the receiver controls whether the feedback is understood, accepted, and adopted."

Lead by example and create a safe environment for your team to speak up without fear of consequences. It's important for leaders to practice what they preach and guide their staff in communication skills. It is important for staff to feel safe sharing their thoughts and worries facing no repercussions.

Set concise rules for respectful communication and address your team's concerns, ensuring fairness in your response. Recognize and reward team members who voice their opinions and acknowledge their efforts. Maintain confidentiality when team members share sensitive information and seek feedback to enhance team communication.

Remember, trust and open communication take time to develop. Work hard and be intentional about creating a safe space so your team can speak their minds and share ideas, which leads to more collaboration, innovation, and overall success.

Consequences of Ignoring Failure.

Failure, when disregarded, has the potential to harm individuals, teams, and organizations. One of the major drawbacks is failing to take advantage of valuable learning opportunities. When we overlook failures, we deprive ourselves of learning and growth opportunities. Disregarding failure obstructs creating new ideas and motivation. Teams may develop a fear of taking risks and become unwilling to try new things. When people don't receive constructive feedback on their errors, they become less involved and responsible.

Ignoring failure can damage an organization's reputation and relationships, and cause stakeholders and the public to lose trust, which reduces business and investor confidence.

Breaking Down the Failure to Feedback Barrier.

As a leader of Marigold Academy, I've learned that not giving feedback to my teachers and administrative staff holds us back and prevents us from growing. Author and business leader Jim Rohn states, "Feedback is what champions have for breakfast." At Marigold Academy, we're not living in a bubble. To improve our staff's skills and meet their needs, we utilize feedback. I've accepted that knowing how to give and receive feedback is an art and a science. However, it only works if both people are on the same page with respect and transparency. If you don't get that right, the feedback won't be as useful and could affect how well it performs. It's all about finding the right balance and creating a culture of honest feedback to help the company. Most important is that feedback is only helpful if it is delivered. This means approaching negative feedback with the right attitude and handling it with kids' gloves is necessary; it all starts with you as a leader.

But how can you turn failure into a learning opportunity for your business and yourself?

Utilizing failure as feedback, I've developed a technique that effectively promotes professional and personal development. As a leader, I encourage my team by showing empathy and understanding. Instructing them on the value of learning from mistakes and failures, I help them make wise choices and progress.

Embrace a Growth Mindset.

In the beginning of this book, I talked about how important it is to have a strong mindset and view failure as an opportunity to grow. Keep in mind that making mistakes is normal while learning; it doesn't define how talented or valuable you are. When you have a growth mindset, challenges become opportunities for learning and personal development.

Analyzing Your Fear of Failure.

The fear of failure haunts many people. To overcome this fear, begin with realistic goal setting, self-compassion, and confronting negative thoughts. Ask for help from a mentor, coworker, relative, or friend. Talking to someone you respect and trust can be a significant change and a massive help for a leader. If you fear your next move or don't understand a big decision, reach out to someone you trust and ask for their advice. There isn't any shame in seeking help from others.

Identify Causes of Failure.

When certain things happen, and you face mistakes of failure, first, take a moment to think about why it didn't work out. Ask yourself if anyone did anything or had any outside influences. If you're afraid of failing, figure out what scares you the most and see if you can handle it. Once you know what you are facing, focus on gaining the confidence to handle whatever comes next. Here are some questions to help you in this situation:

- Which of these outcomes most worries you?
- To what extent will they affect you?
- Are they only uncomfortable or potentially fatal?
- How soon will you let go?
- Are the effects irreversible or permanent?
- Will they pass quickly or remain for a very long time?
- Can you manage them well enough?
- Will you hide and run away, or can you control the damage?

It's not the absence of fear that makes you fearless, but your belief in your ability to handle the outcomes of your decisions.

Gather Feedback from Trusted Others.

I've talked about this earlier and honestly believe that finding mentors who share your interests is a wise decision. Every week, I meet a corporate leadership coach and mentor who offers me invaluable advice. Connect with a mentor who has the expertise and know-how to support you in accomplishing your objectives. Swallow your pride and ask for advice from colleagues, mentors, or coworkers when needed.

As your franchisor, I can always answer your questions and help you through challenging times. That's what I do. A mentor like me can help you level up your systems and find solutions. When you step up, put your pride aside, and ask for the help of others, you will soon be confident enough to handle things you never imagined. Getting a fresh perspective can be super helpful when you're stuck and don't know what to do.

Develop an Action Plan from Feedback.

Leaders must collect feedback prior to developing an action plan. Having a comprehensive plan outlining your company's future goals is vital for executives and business owners. When creating your action plan, evaluate behaviors, skills, and talents to ensure they match your company's goals, purposes, and core values.

Use feedback to your advantage to figure out what's not working and take a step back and change your approach. Create a plan that helps you to move forward and achieve your goals.

Implement Changes

To keep growing, it's important to implement improvements by taking what you've learned from your mistakes. Make those slight changes and place them into your action plan to reach bigger goals, stay on track and avoid getting lost or deviating from your company's direction plan.

Reflect and Adjust.

From your feedback, take moments to see how far you've come with your goals. Are the tweaks doing their job? Is everything still on track? If not, what can you adjust to stay on course with your team and business? Stay open to change and be ready to adjust your approach depending on what's working and what's not.

Stay the Course.

Don't forget, it takes patience and perseverance to make tangible progress. Always keep moving forward and never stop learning from failures, especially as leaders. A good leader knows they can always get better. These steps can turn failure into a useful tool for personal growth.

Our Marigold Academy franchise allows our incredible staff to rise into corporate leadership roles. Upward career mobility is only available by learning and being open-minded to new ways to improve while supporting personal legacies. "Two heads are better than one," British author C.S. Lewis said a lot. "Not because one is perfect, but because they are less likely to go wrong at the same time." The point of this quote is that we should all work together and learn from each other when giving feedback.

I've seen firsthand how the failure-to-feedback cycle is significant and seen my company break free from destructive patterns, providing a refreshing and supportive atmosphere across every Marigold Academy. Simon Sinek said, "Failure is a great teacher, and if you are open to it, every mistake has a lesson to offer." This culture of continuous learning and open communication fosters such an environment.

In business and franchising, overcoming the fear of failure means changing the company's culture, making failure less taboo, encouraging open communication, and fostering a culture of continuous learning. According to Robert Kiyosaki, "Don't let the fear of losing outweigh the excitement of winning." Remember this as you go through the challenges of being an entrepreneur or a new franchisee.

When you see failure to succeed and make a safe space for people to share and give feedback, you give yourself and your team the tools to learn and grow, even when mistakes happen. Believe in the process and use feedback to make things even better. Watch your business thrive as it embraces a culture of resilience, collaboration, and innovative ideas. In case you forget, Winston Churchill said, "Success is not final, failure is not fatal: it is the courage to continue that counts."

***

Important Points

- Setting up a safe space for open conversation and feedback not only helps each person grow but also helps the team succeed.
- In business, feedback is the lifeblood of growth and improvement.
- Feedback is how companies and individuals learn, adapt, and innovate.
- As leaders, constructive criticism is not only polite but essential for team development and achievement.
- Leaders should know how important it is to give constructive feedback to break free from this negative cycle and ensure the receiver understands what you mean.
- Give your staff positive feedback so they can learn from their mistakes and make progress.

Chapter 6:

Working in Your Genius Zone

"Genius is one percent inspiration and ninety-nine percent perspiration." ~ **Thomas Edison**

Ernest Hemingway, born in Oak Park, Illinois, in 1899, had little desire to pursue a career in writing. He took part in the high school journalism club, igniting his interest in writing as a student. However, following high school, Hemingway volunteered to drive ambulances for the American Red Cross during World War I.

This event shaped his writing style and worldview, which was replete with the brutal realities of battle; after the war, Hemingway started a career in journalism. Here, under the guidance of the newspaper's style guide, which emphasized lively English and a powerful, upbeat tone—elements that later became hallmarks of his literary work—Hemingway refined his writing style.

In 1920, he went to Paris, a center for foreign writers and the avant-garde, following his heart, a crucial action. His encounters with notable writers such as F. Scott Fitzgerald and Gertrude Stein in Paris influenced the development of his writing style. He battled alcoholism and four failed marriages but overcame severe personal hardships to pursue his passion for writing, find his genius, and earn the Nobel Prize in Literature.

He received this in 1954 for his portrayal of an elderly fisherman's quest for a massive marlin in *The Old Man and the Sea*, which is a potent and beautiful story. This was the pinnacle of his body of work, given in recognition of his mastery of the narrative form and his impact on modern style.

Ernest Hemingway's story is a potent testament that finding one's calling can sometimes be gradual, influenced as much by personal experiences as by innate talents. His life and work are classic examples of finding passion and a Zone of Genius through knowledge and perseverance. His approach to literature was transformative, influencing countless writers and the broader literary landscape.

Have you ever considered your Zone of Genius? Have you considered what excites you? When you discover your passion and strive to reach your full potential, you are in your Zone of Genius. You may be wondering how discovering your passion can benefit you as a new franchisee.

***

Vignette: Personal Note from Gary Occhiogrosso

When Jay Shah first contacted me, he came to me by way of a friendly competitor, Steve Begelman from SMB Franchise Advisors, who created manuals and systems documentation for his franchise work. Knowing Steve's reputation in the industry, I knew Jay Shah was a serious-minded individual. What impressed me the most was that Jay was a strong entrepreneur, and he and his wife came into the childcare industry with the right mindset. Jay took the time to understand everything about the industry with a methodical engineer's mindset and architect approach.

***

As Chief Executive Officer of Marigold Academy, my career path leading to Marigold Academy was an unexpected one. After a decade and a half in corporate jobs, I found my passion and talent for early childhood education in 2019. Though I lacked experience, I could only think about my vision for creating nurturing environments for young minds. After discovering how much I enjoy nurturing young minds and building businesses, I knew that was my calling and started the journey to turn Marigold Academy into an esteemed institution that not only enriches young minds but also provides a platform for teachers and aspiring entrepreneurs to reach their true potential. I was confident that franchising was the direction I wanted to go in, and I wondered how it would bring about a change in my life. I believed that franchising could enhance my life and the lives of those around me.

That urge was deep-seated, and my soon-to-be Zone of Genius would not quit inside me. Unable to tolerate the 'what if' any longer, I made the decision to act and ensure I wouldn't have any regrets down the line. I confided in my wife and family about what truly matters to me. I sought advice from both my mentors and franchising experts. We spoke about the substantial financial commitment and personal sacrifices that were necessary to make my dream come true. She understood, seeing my passion, and agreed, pushing me to follow my gut and shoot for my dreams and legacy.

The Zone of Genius theory, popularized by Gay Hendricks in his book *The Big Leap*, refers to the state where individuals work from their innate strengths and do what they love. It's the perfect blend of your strengths and passions, resulting in exceptional performance and deep satisfaction in your work. Realizing your full potential in life is important. But once you do, you will have laid the groundwork for a prosperous future. Colonel Sanders, who created KFC at age 65, realized the power, passion, and genius behind his ability to create wonderful fried chicken. Everybody experiences it in their lives; some experience it earlier in life, while others experience it later.

Achieving your full potential results from living up to your potential. Then comes the hustle, and the great thing is that it doesn't seem laborious when this happens. Even after a demanding day, you feel fulfilled when you put all your effort into something you're passionate about. Even if things don't go as planned, your happiness can be akin to a life without regrets. Without realizing your potential, it's difficult to envision the happiness, achievement, and strong bonds that await in your life.

When you realize your true potential, a new world of opportunities opens up beyond what you imagined. With business or franchising, the first step is to identify your Zone of Genius through self-assessment and introspection. Identifying and implementing your strengths in the childcare sector can contribute to your success as a franchisee. Begin with these essential steps:

Reflect on Your Experiences: Think about your professional and personal past experiences. Consider the tasks and roles where you excelled and found the most satisfaction. By experiencing these, you can uncover your natural strengths.

Take a Personality or Strengths Assessment: Many online tools, such as the Myers-Briggs Type Indicator (MBTI), StrengthsFinder, AQme Assessment, or The Wheel of Life, can help you identify your strengths and personality traits. These assessments give you a glimpse into your communication style, problem-solving skills, and leadership traits.

Seek Feedback from Others: Ask friends, family, colleagues, or mentors what they perceive as your strengths. They may offer valuable perspectives you hadn't considered. Discuss your goals with people you trust. Tell them what's on your heart, then listen to their response. You'll be surprised by the value you'll receive from those who care about you. That will not only bring clarity but also inspire you with better ideas than you could have thought of alone.

Align Your Strengths with Childcare: Think about the ways you can use your skills to manage a childcare franchise. Are you a strong communicator? Do you have passion for children and early education? Are you a good leader? Compassion and excellent communication skills make interaction with parents and staff easier and less challenging in a childcare franchise. As a natural leader, you can motivate and empower your team to provide excellent care for the children.

Develop Your Strengths: Once you've identified your strengths, invest time and resources into further developing them. Attend workshops, read books, or seek mentorship to enhance the skills that will contribute to your success as a childcare franchisee. Through the discovery and utilization of your strengths, you have the power to affect children and families in your community.

For new franchise owners, tapping into your Zone of Genius is a strategic move for business growth. Leveraging your Zone of Genius starts by aligning tasks with your personal strengths. Guaranteeing this alignment ensures that you invest your time where it matters most, resulting in better results. Our culture supports and values individual genius zones, motivating team members to find and work within their area of expertise. As famous basketball coach Phil Jackson said, "The strength of the team is each member. The strength of each member is the team."

Our staff at Marigold Academy have excelled in their work and careers using this model. It not just improves individual performance, but also strengthens team synergy and productivity. Author Peter Drucker said, "The most successful organizations don't make a better person out of everyone; they build on each person's unique strengths and ensure that weaknesses become irrelevant." Leaders who acknowledge and use their team's individual strengths can discover innovative breakthroughs and solutions they may not have achieved on their own.

To make the most of your time in your Zone of Genius, I recommend you develop and personalize your role as a new franchise owner within the Marigold Academy franchise. Assign tasks to others to help you stay on track and maintain focus.

Build a business that cultivates an environment aligned with your expertise. Team building and ongoing support for our staff and leaders are crucial attributes that our model is based on. We only hire people whose areas of expertise align with ours. This method enables you to build a team that is balanced and lets you focus on your areas of expertise.

Tapping into your area of expertise fuels growth. Enhance your expertise by investing in personal and professional development. As you become more experienced as a franchisee, look for expansion opportunities that allow you to build upon your strengths. Explore new fields where your unique talents can excel.

Once you understand these variables, use KPIs to ensure that working in your Zone of Genius yields measurable results. At this stage, it's crucial to stay flexible and adjust your tactics as you progress.

Unique Value Proposition.

When my wife and I joined the early childhood education industry in 2019, we understood the significance of adopting a holistic approach to early education. Our special quality lies in making children feel at home as we prepare them for a future of accomplishment. Besides those principles, we prioritized age-specific programs that combine academics and social-emotional learning to foster confidence and skills. It was our Unique Value Proposition (UVP), and we now use it to guide our franchisees every step of the way.

Prior to owning a childcare business, I worked in finance and excelled in managing both finances and people. That was what set me apart and made me stand out. However, I wasn't born with that. Throughout the past twenty years, I have explored various areas and taken on different roles, such as engineering, operations, project management, finance, and accounting.

Through diversifying my career, I have developed the ability to perform at my highest level. My success as a franchisor stems from my skill in guiding franchisees towards optimal performance and offering comprehensive support in all aspects of their business.

Marigold Academy is the preferred choice for parents seeking childcare as our teachers are joyful, committed, and passionate about providing exceptional care, enabling parents to have peace of mind. That is the Marigold philosophy and culture that drives our brands, reputation, and success.

You may be asking, now that you're here, what's my UVP? How do I find it? It starts with real-world self-reflection. Being alone in your thoughts is the surefire way to discover what makes you stand out. Taking time to reflect is important as it helps you gain a better understanding of yourself and what makes you valuable. Think about self-reflection as your way of looking into a mirror to see yourself more clearly. Doing this lets you learn who you are, what you're capable of, and what you stand for. You must be honest with yourself and make sure you are reflecting on what is yours. Don't think about things others may want you to do or offer. When you're self-aware of who you are, you make better decisions, communicate more effectively, and build stronger relationships.

Another way to identify your unique value is by being aware and understanding what others need or want. Knowing this, you can use your unique value proposition to combine your skills, experiences, and qualities that can benefit others in a way that makes you stand out.

Part of owning a franchise is defining and applying your core values to your business. A UVP should outline what makes your franchise business, product, or service distinctive and valuable to your families. It differentiates you from the competition, showcasing your specific value.

Ask yourself what core values drive your business or personal brand. These values should resonate through your services or products, influencing your business practices and understanding customer needs and wants.

As a franchisor and business leader, I understand how to align with your personal value and what you bring to the table. Marigold Academy's support extends to targeted marketing strategies, extensive hiring and operations training, and ongoing mentoring to deliver exceptional enrichment programs in local communities.

It was our novelty, our differentiator, and as a business, that unique value was one of the main things that drove the intake of students and continuous growth. You must offer better and superior services to stand out from the crowd. Reflect on your area of expertise and ensure it aligns with kindergarten readiness, a nurturing environment, experienced and compassionate teachers, minimal staff turnover, consistent and high-quality care, and improved teacher-to-child ratios. These translate into happy children, teachers, and parents. Remember, building loyalty and value is hard, so think long term and don't take shortcuts.

Knowing what your customers want is key, and as a franchisee, you have to highlight what makes you stand out. What do you offer above the competition? What do you bring to the table that no one else can? This could be exceptional customer service, an innovative childcare program, or improved health and safety measures. Whatever that is, articulate that into your UVP. Do whatever it takes to make sure parents, children, and staff understand and connect with the value.

Limiting Beliefs.

A few things can hinder your franchise's progress, and one of the key factors is limiting belief in yourself and leadership. Self-doubt can be substantial. I struggled with this as I was uncertain how to lead Marigold Academy successfully. Yes, I had doubts, but I worked hard, reached out to experts for advice, and trusted in myself as a person and leader to reach my potential. As a parent, I understood and resonated with other parents' frustrations and needs. Parents want to have security, knowing that their children are well taken care of and in excellent hands, happy and thriving.

We ensure parents these things by providing our teachers with healthy and stress-free environments to work in. Happy teachers cultivate happy children, and happy children cultivate happy parents. That is the Marigold philosophy.

However, if the environment and your actions make families doubt and feel insecure, that can affect you personally as a new franchisee in several ways.

If you're scared or unsure, you might end up putting things off. Are you this person? Are you afraid to get started and are stuck behind the gate? I've witnessed it unfold when individuals are paralyzed by the fear of failure. If you're afraid of taking risks, you might pass up on some amazing opportunities. But as author Marianne Williamson reminded us, "Our deepest fear is not that we are inadequate. Our deepest fear is that we are powerful beyond measure."

As a franchisee, please do your best to identify any fears and beliefs that could hinder progress and sort them out. As a new franchisee, you have to break through self-imposed limits and see them for what they are: just beliefs, not truths.

Limiting beliefs can kill your motivation, making you not want to try to succeed if you think it won't make a difference. Want to be successful? Just shift your mindset by thinking positively and getting rid of negative thoughts.

Look at what's going on and fix it. It's good to talk to other franchisees or successful business leaders. Have a conversation with people who have overcome similar struggles. In addition to other franchisees, find mentors who can give advice, feedback, and support.

Changing your mindset with a new perspective can be done. But it will take conscious effort. If you stay positive and see challenges as opportunities, you'll learn and grow. If you want to tap into your Genius Zone, deal with and overcome your self-doubt. This may involve reframing negative thoughts, seeking support from friends and mentors, or practicing self-compassion. Remember, as writer Anaïs Nin said, "Life shrinks or expands in proportion to one's courage."

Through the use of these approaches, you can dismantle restrictive beliefs and elevate your confidence and potential to capitalize on your current franchise opportunities with Marigold Academy. Lead fearlessly, exceed business goals, and unleash your full potential by embracing strategic risk-taking and focusing on your passion and expertise.

Embracing your expertise makes your life and business better. It's the way to incredible success and happiness. Finding and nurturing your unique talents is the first step to achieving long-term success. Now is the time to do it.

***

Important Points

- Do your best to overcome procrastination or fear by changing your thinking and mindset with a new perspective.
- Shifting your mindset to be positive in all your efforts will help you view challenges as opportunities and failures as feedback in the long term, helping you learn and grow.
- Coordinate your Zone of Genius with your franchise business.
- Make the most of your time in your Zone of Genius by cultivating and customizing your role within the Marigold Academy franchise.
- Tapping into your Zone of Genius isn't just about personal fulfillment; it's a strategic move for business growth.
- Leveraging your Zone of Genius for business success starts with aligning tasks with your strengths.

Chapter 7:

Franchising Leadership Adaptability, Change and Agility

"Exercising adaptive leadership is about giving meaning to your life beyond your own ambition." ~ **Ronald Heifetz,** ***The Practice of Adaptive Leadership: Tools and Tactics for Changing Your Organization and the World***

In 2014, Satya Nadella took over as Microsoft's CEO, stepping into a tough market where they were lagging in essential areas like AI, mobile, and cloud computing. Before Nadella took charge, Microsoft focused on traditional business strategies and products like desktop operating systems and office applications. Stepping in with an adaptable mindset, Nadella welcomed AI and embraced the cloud, where he recognized the changing tech market and adjusted the company's focus.

He realized that cloud services and AI technologies drive growth, so he endorsed their progress and adoption. It was a risky decision that transformed the business's operations, investments, and focus. By fostering creativity and teamwork, he helped to reshape Microsoft's corporate culture and product strategy. He transformed the previous competitive and isolated setting into a more accessible and cooperative work environment. He prioritized empathy, learning from errors, and fostering innovation in his leadership.

Under Nadella's guidance, Microsoft experienced a remarkable resurgence, dominating the cloud computing industry with Azure, a powerful competitor to Amazon's AWS. This strategic realignment revitalized the company's growth and elevated its market worth. The change also enabled Microsoft to develop innovative AI and machine learning solutions. Nadella's leadership has brought about a cultural shift that has boosted staff morale and output. By prioritizing teamwork and collaboration, the company achieved a more committed staff and introduced inventive goods and solutions. Many consider his management approach—and Microsoft's achievements under his leadership—to be standout examples of adaptability and flexibility to modern technology.

Being adaptable as a leader means surviving and thriving through changes and turning challenges into opportunities. Leaders who possess this quality can navigate their organizations through uncertainties and motivate their teams by demonstrating unwavering strength and proactive problem-solving in the face of challenges. Leaders in franchising need to be adaptable, and that includes you.

Success requires adapting and changing course as the business shifts. Jim Collins, author of *Good to Great*, believes that successful companies are those that face harsh reality and make hard choices when confronted with change. It's the same in franchising. Refusing to change and having a stale business strategy is a disaster in the making. If you want the business to succeed, you must adapt and revise your plans.

***

Vignette: Personal Note from Gary Occhiogrosso

I quickly learned the difference between the work of the franchising business. It is a business model geared toward improving the lives of teams, staff, and employees. Franchising, as a development tool and business model, I believe, is the greatest business model ever created in the history of the United States. And why do I say that? This is because most businesses in the United States are small businesses, and not every business owner is Mark Zuckerberg or Elon Musk.

***

But how can you, as a franchise leader, change your business strategies when needed? It all starts with being open-minded, flexible, and ready to learn. As a leader, be humble and encourage collaboration and feedback from your team. Be open to trying new strategies if things aren't working out. Stay in the loop about industry trends and customer needs and adapt.

You, as a leader, can benefit from seeking outside expertise and guidance, such as from consultants or mentors. I'm a big fan of mentors and coaches helping me navigate new surroundings and the business world. The knowledge I get from my coaching sessions with my mentors is key to the success of our work at the Marigold Academy. Besides mentors, an important thing is being able to adapt to change and approach challenges with a growth mindset.

In regular leadership models, only a handful of people are in control. Asking for advice from others is common, but authority and hierarchy take precedence. Adaptive leaders value and consider everyone's beliefs and ideas, not just those of company leaders.

Adaptive leadership was all the rage in the 90s and early 2000s. The core principles were established by authors Ronald Heifetz, Marty Linksy, and Alexander Grashow in books like *Leadership Without Easy Answers* and *Leadership on the Line*. With our working lives getting more complicated, adaptive leadership is more relevant than ever. Scholars like Nick Obolensky say it's the only way to stay afloat in today's crazy business world.

Giving staff ongoing training and development opportunities helps your franchise build an adaptive culture. When my wife and I had twins and began looking for childcare, we discovered the significance of a comfortable second home for children. I made it clear what we wanted for our children. We wanted a home away from home for our children, where they could develop physically, emotionally, and intellectually.

After touring dozens of childcare centers near where we lived, we could find no place that felt like a second home. Instead, we saw a commercial and impersonal situation, where every child was just treated as a number and dollar sign for the owners. This was discouraging. That's when it hit us—we could create a superior model by giving children and parents the care they deserve. And that's how Marigold Academy came to be.

Offering ongoing training and development opportunities for our staff played a big role in building a flexible culture. Making sure kids are well taken care of in early childhood education allows parents to focus on work and family. It's all about the amazing teachers and staff.

At Marigold Academy, we ensure that our teachers have a happy and nurturing environment. We offer them competitive pay, reliable schedules, and a healthy work-life balance. Quality is important to us, and we ensure that classrooms are adequately staffed. Our number of teachers surpasses the state's requirements for caring for children.

With additional teachers, children receive better care and development, giving parents a sense of safety and security. Parents will pay extra tuition fees if more teachers attend to their children. Additional teachers result in improved care, increased engagement, and enhanced focus during lunch, snack, and nap times.

Enhanced monitoring and observation contribute to a safer outdoor setting for kids. With additional staff, the work environment becomes less stressful as more support is available.

Our ability to embrace change catalyzed our belief that teachers and staff were the backbone of our new childcare center. At Marigold Academy, our newfound philosophy became simple: happy teachers cultivate happy children. The happiness of parents is connected to the happiness of their children. It all has synergy and goes hand-in-hand.

Childcare goes beyond mere extravagant buildings and attention-grabbing promotions. There's something else. Although all those things may seem attractive, the accurate measure of a successful childcare model rests on the satisfaction and growth potential of its teachers and staff. Our organization is revolutionizing the childcare industry.

***

Vignette: Personal Note About Franchising—Gary Occhiogrosso

With franchising, when you walk into a McDonald's, for example, McDonald's corporate office doesn't sell anything. They don't sell hamburgers. Instead, they sell a system that people use. They license the ability to use their system to sell hamburgers and is the cash flow vehicle where corporate collects a royalty.

***

Management expert Peter Drucker once said, "Knowledge has become the key economic resource and the dominant, if not the only, source of competitive advantage." When leaders prioritize staff training, their organizations are better prepared for any changes, adapt, and drive innovation. I see this every day; teachers and staff feel encouraged to approach my wife and I with new ideas, all in the name of improving the Marigold Academy. Whether I use the ideas or not, I feel proud that my staff knows they can approach me without fear of ridicule or being shut down. I remain open and flexible, which is an important trait as a franchise owner.

***

Vignette: Personal Note from Kruti Shah

We try to hire internally, feeling it is best to stick with people with childcare experience and those that understand Marigold culture. We give opportunities internally to the people to improve loyalty and satisfaction. It's the best way. Jay and I are always looking for ways to provide challenging and better opportunities for our top performers.

***

The flexibility to thrive in various positions is key to your organization's success. To achieve staff training and development, it is important to adopt a range of methods that accommodate different learning styles and organizational needs. To get started, consider on-the-job orientation and training, which involves teachers and staff working with experienced colleagues and receiving real-time guidance and feedback. By utilizing this hands-on approach, your staff can gain practical skills while participating in the company's daily operations. Everyone comes out ahead.

Your interactive sessions with staff could be workshops, seminars, and/or industry conferences, offering another way to learn and develop specific topics or skills. These events allow staff to learn and engage with specific topics/material. Online courses and e-learning also provide flexible options for employees to access training materials at their own convenience and pace.

I believe in mentors and advice from professional experts. The one thing has let me grow as a leader, husband, and father. Personalized support and advice from experienced mentors or coaches in mentoring and coaching programs foster one-on-one learning. Cross-functional training exposes employees to different departments or roles, broadening their understanding of the organization and helping them develop new skills. It also serves as a backup if current staff leave your business. All these things in your franchise will be a big change in improving your Marigold Academy.

Much like any business, embracing change in franchising means reacting to what's happening outside and trying to improve within the organization. American author John C. Maxwell said, "Change is inevitable. Growth is optional." By motivating your team to embrace change and develop a growth mindset, you can build a workforce that is resilient. The ability to adapt and be flexible is vital for franchise owners and leaders in the evolving business of franchising. Leaders who embrace new ideas and adapt their strategies can ensure the competitiveness and success of their businesses.

Adaptability fuels leaders to tackle unforeseen obstacles, such as sudden market changes or the rise of fresh rivals and competition. It helps them take advantage of new opportunities as well. By being adaptable, you, as a new franchise owner, can foster a culture of innovation and collaboration. Promote staff participation in sharing ideas and feedback, showcasing your dedication to learning and development and setting a positive example as a leader fostering a culture of ongoing improvement.

Your success in the franchise world hinges on your capacity for versatility. As a leader, roll with the punches, be willing to change course and be able to expect and prepare for future challenges. When I stepped into the world of childcare, I faced many challenges. Instead of letting it get to me or making me want to quit, I pushed through, adapted to what I had, and made it work.

My inexperience meant listening to staff and families first. I enhanced our facilities to prioritize health and safety, stimulated young minds with STEM, sign language, and foreign language programs, and fostered diversity and inclusion. By implementing a culture that empowers remarkable teachers, we cultivate excellence in every child.

In 2021, an opportunity arose to expand Marigold Academy with a second location. With our proven model, we brought in adaptive and caring staff, improved our facilities and curriculums, and aligned our operations to ensure families could trust us, no matter where we're located.

However, the second school we acquired was facing challenges, so we turned it into a thriving center by providing home-away-from-home care, a well-rounded curriculum, and prioritizing happy teachers. Our revenue and profitability skyrocketed in just a few years. Our successful business turnaround was driven by our compassionate approach, adaptability, and growing enrollment as local families spread positive referrals in the community.

Adaptable leadership means being able to turn a vision into reality. A successful franchise relies on a clear vision and the ability to adapt as circumstances change. Smart leaders can juggle long-term goals and short-term needs, making decisions that set their organizations up for success even in uncertain times. Fostering a constant learning culture helps your franchise organization stay ahead. It's a fast-paced market, and business magnate Richard Branson stated, "Every success story is a tale of constant adaptation, revision, and change."

In the world of franchising, customer preferences are always shifting, so being adaptable is crucial. As a new franchise owner, taking risks, thinking, and experimenting with new ideas is essential to stay in the game. Former General Electric CEO Jack Welch said, "Willingness to change is a strength, even if it means plunging part of the company into total confusion for a while." But being adaptable isn't just about quick decision-making when things go wrong. Investing in ongoing staff training equips your staff to handle anything.

Skill enhancement programs work like magic in helping your team adjust to new processes and technologies. Plus, investing in your employees' growth helps them prepare for the future and creates a culture of continuous learning in your organization.

People are not fond of change, which makes it difficult to make changes. People naturally oppose anything that is different. Often, facing different things leads to negative emotional responses. This is the moment for you, as a leader, to step up. Keeping team morale up for the franchise to thrive is super important. When staff feel appreciated and have support, they're happier and more motivated at work.

My wife and I promote a supportive work environment through our open-door policy for our staff. We strive to sustain and nurture team morale and satisfaction. It's vital for new leaders to recognize and appreciate the hard work of their team members. A simple "thank you" or a word of appreciation can achieve boosting team morale and fostering a strong team dynamic.

Low morale can harm productivity and employee retention. When team members become disengaged and unmotivated or feel unappreciated or undervalued, this can lead to poor performance and impact the business's success. You must address any issues affecting morale and create a supportive work environment where employees feel empowered and motivated to do their best work.

Success in franchising requires leaders to be adaptable, embrace change, and lead with agility. By embracing change and leading with agility, you can stay ahead and overcome challenges. Albert Einstein said, "The measure of intelligence is the ability to change. "Support employee growth through skill enhancement programs, encourage a positive company culture, and promote teamwork to maintain high morale. Doing this will benefit your business and establish a solid foundation for long-term success in the Marigold Academy franchise.

***

Important Points

- Success in franchising requires leaders to be adaptable, embrace change, and have agility.
- The essence of adaptability in leadership lies in surviving changes, thriving through them, and turning potential threats into opportunities.
- In the franchising world, consumer preferences always change, so being agile is key.
- As a new franchise owner, you must take risks, think creatively, and experiment with new ideas to stay in the game.
- When staff feel appreciated and have support, they're happier and more motivated at work.

- Even in the face of adversity, leaders can show unyielding resilience, guiding their organizations through uncertain times and inspiring their teams with their proactive approach to challenges.
- Listen to your staff and customers for constant improvement.

Chapter 8:

Overcoming Fear and Self-doubt in the Franchise World

"Inaction breeds doubt and fear. Action breeds confidence and courage. If you want to conquer fear, do not sit at home and think about it. Go out and get busy." ~ **Dale Carnegie.**

S erena Williams, born on September 26, 1981, in Saginaw, Michigan, showed exceptional talent in tennis from a young age. Growing up in Compton, California, a neighborhood known for its high crime and poverty, Serena faced and overcame racism, sexism, and self-doubt. Her rigorous training regimen and the support of her father, Richard Williams, played a pivotal role in nurturing this talent and overcoming all those emotional challenges. Since arriving on the scene at 13 years old at the Bell Challenge in Quebec, the 23-time Grand Slam champion has endured more than her fair share of blatant mistreatment and racist onslaughts.

Serena acknowledged, "Before a match, I still have a lot of self-doubts...a tremendous amount of nerves." Despite this, when Williams enters the court, spectators witness the ultimate expression of confidence and determination. "My greatest strength is my mental game," said Williams. Serena's legacy inspires many, demonstrating that success is possible by overcoming self-doubt and facing fears and challenges. Her story underscores the importance of perseverance, resilience, and the continuous fight for equality worldwide.

In franchising and entrepreneurship, leaders must acknowledge the significant influence of fear and self-doubt on personal and professional growth. Fear, as we all know, is a powerful emotion. When something unfamiliar is put in front of us, or when we feel threatened, we experience worry and unease. There is science behind it. It has everything to do with your brain and the 'fight or flight' response. This is a natural physiological reaction to something you and I see as stressful or frightening. It is a natural way our bodies respond to fear in this way to prepare for the threat.

In franchising, fear does not stop the heart or pose a threat. Fear can take many forms, such as financial loss, insecurity, lack of confidence, fear of failure, or anxiety about meeting expectations. Fear has its advantages. And despite these things, it keeps you on your toes. It pushes you to learn and understand yourself, fostering continual self-improvement.

When I first decided to go into franchising, I was excited. I had never been so enthusiastic about the possibilities. Upon doing my due diligence, speaking with industry experts and consultants, and learning from other franchisors, I realized how hard, time-consuming, and costly this venture would be. I got cold feet. Fear took over, and it was so bad I put the project on hold. Almost a year passed, and not a single day passed without me thinking about franchising.

The idea of the opportunities I would have to learn and grow, the legacy I would build for my family, and how many lives (children, teachers, and entrepreneurs) would change because of my actions. What would have been the alternative if I hadn't taken that action? For example, if I hadn't left engineering and finance, I would have stayed put, gone through the motions of life, and spent many days in my old life wondering 'what if'... That was enough for me to snap out of it and take on the challenge head-on. I spent the next year learning from industry experts and other franchisors, honing my skills, obtaining the financing to support this huge venture, and then I took the plunge.

New franchisees often struggle with a lack of confidence in their abilities, skills, and decision-making, which I see as a major issue as a leader. It's typical and expected, especially for someone who is new. If this is you, the key is to do your best to face the doubt by recognizing the symptoms and taking action to remove it from your life. Strive to ease symptoms like negative thoughts, avoiding challenges, feeling overwhelmed, and confusion between caution and unproductive doubt. While self-doubt is common, you should deal with excessive self-doubt by practicing self-compassion, using coping strategies, seeking social support, and seeking professional help if necessary.

Are you doubting yourself by talking negatively and comparing yourself to the failures and others? Are recent changes stopping you dead in your tracks? If so, you need to shift your mindset and believe in yourself. Once you do that, you can take control of your emotional self-doubt, bounce back, and make your business thrive.

Never underestimate the importance of dealing with self-doubt and fear in franchising because, if ignored, they can lead to decision hesitation, uncertainty, and lack of assertiveness.

As a franchisee, fear and self-doubt can hold you back from progress and hinder your ability to seize new opportunities, take risks, expand your business, or implement innovative ideas that enhance success and profitability. Ignoring fear and self-doubt can have a detrimental impact on both your leadership and your team's success.

Self-doubt was paralyzing when I launched Marigold Academy. As someone unfamiliar with the childcare industry, fear filled me. To build my confidence, I started conducting thorough research. I went to various daycare facilities. During my conversations with numerous childcare center owners, I discussed both the challenges they face and the positive experiences they have had. I educated myself to eliminate my fears one at a time.

Acting on good advice is the most effective approach to overcoming fear and self-doubt, and this can be achieved by seeking guidance from industry leaders, mentors, and trusted individuals while learning as much as possible.

Through action and learning from others, I've changed my mindset and turned negatives into positives. Self-doubt is something everyone experiences. It's in our DNA. The key is to uncover the root of the cause and do your best to understand what is causing you to feel insecure.

Self-doubt's biggest problem is that it causes you to second-guess decisions. As a leader, I know that firsthand; doubt almost killed our dreams, even after we started our first Marigold Academy. Actor Tom Hanks said, "Our greatest weapon against all enemies is our unwavering courage that we refuse to give up." That statement resonated with me and my wife. We knew we were walking into the unknown. I had a strong inner conviction that we could achieve success, and that motivation helped me push through my doubts and fears. My determination to create an exceptional childcare center surpassed my fears and doubts, and I used it to my advantage.

When you experience self-doubt, it can have a detrimental effect on your work environment and communication with your staff, leading to a loss of trust and rapport as a leader. To ensure everyone is on the same page, create a positive environment by being open to new ideas from your staff. This creates an inviting atmosphere, helping you keep staff where everyone feels comfortable, respected, and supported.

At Marigold Academy, we prioritize comprehensive support for our staff in every way. Our philosophy is that a happy staff fosters a productive and collaborative work environment. From the beginning, we saw how self-doubt created high levels of stress, anxiety, and burnout, which can damage the mental health and well-being of everyone. We knew we had to develop a method and company mission that always supported staff and ensured a stress-free and positive work environment.

Regardless of your new franchise's status, acknowledging weaknesses is crucial for achieving success. It takes grit and guts to admit shortcomings, and I understand. Yet, along with your shortcomings, it is also essential to improve upon your strengths. It all goes hand-in-hand because if you don't know where to improve, enhancing your work performance and advancing your career is impossible.

It is vital to maintain balance with self-awareness. If you fixate too much on your flaws and neglect to recognize your unique contributions, you risk missing out on the beauty of your potential to lead your company to success.

You're human, and common fears often hold you back, like the fear of failure or of letting others down. Fear is a good thing. It keeps you on your toes. It forces you to learn new things and helps you understand yourself better so you can improve yourself.

Maybe you have concerns about losing respect from your family or peers or being incompetent. Primal fears, like feeling marginalized, rejected, or incapable of self-sufficiency, are fear-based emotions that define our humanity to varying degrees. Those fears can stop you in your tracks if you let them. However, every one of us experiences doubt and fear; there isn't any getting around it. According to Robert Kegan and Lisa Laskow Lahey, authors of *Immunity to Change*, "Fear is a constant companion for many individuals, even those who are successful and capable." The problem with fear is that it comes with negative thoughts that are both conscious and unconscious, hindering us from moving forward and hindering our career growth.

When I started Marigold Academy, my biggest fear was not knowing what I was doing. I knew I lacked experience, and doubt crept in about what I was doing. Would I do it right? Could I make this company grow? I had many doubts about whether I was heading in the right direction. It was overwhelming. Yet, I vowed never to let it stop me. I took action to learn all that I could and applied those principles to make the company thrive. I beat self-doubt and feeling inadequate.

Self-doubt and fear are common, especially when you lack experience, skills, or resources, encounter setbacks or failures, and feel pressured to meet specific goals or targets. It's normal to feel worried when you think of those fear-based emotions. When in doubt about taking the chance, think about the alternative. When you fear failure, go back to your WHY. Why are you doing this? What got you motivated, to begin with, before fear took over? Will you be happy with settling for the alternative?

I put a lot of thought into launching Marigold Academy. But I was confused, so I reflected on my life and wondered what it would be like if I didn't pursue the dream. After deep and careful thought, I realized my life would never be right; I had to make a move.

This taught me that the key to dealing with doubts is facing them head-on and acting. Lots of people interested in franchising stress about not having enough experience or skills to run a successful franchise.

I'm here to provide support and help you understand you have the ability to do this.

It's vital not to allow doubt to impede your pursuit of success and happiness. When you hit a wall, talk to a mentor or coach or seek resources and support networks. Construct a solid network of contacts and collaborators to defeat doubt in your world. You must know your weaknesses and flaws and seek proper help, such as coaching or mentoring, to improve. While you may never excel in some areas because of your natural ability and weaknesses, you can gain an edge by learning to control and balance them with your strengths. At Marigold Academy, I take pride in mentoring all franchisees, giving real-world guidance and directives to ensure your success.

Overcoming doubt and fear in franchising involves committing to personal growth and continuous learning. Develop your knowledge and skills through constant learning to use resources like training programs, online courses, and industry literature. By gaining industry-related skills and knowledge, you can diminish feelings of inadequacy and negative thoughts while equipping yourself for success.

Along with acknowledging negative thought patterns in yourself, a leader needs to observe and address them in their team members to promote a productive work atmosphere.

For instance, Sharon, a new childcare center director, doubted herself as she struggled to give successful tours and fill the enrollment. She was questioning herself, trying to figure out what she was doing wrong and why she couldn't convince her parents about their childcare program. Sharon's negative thoughts affected her growth and the team's performance.

Putting yourself as the leader in this scenario to resolve the problem, it's essential to focus on the root cause. Helping Sharon address her negative self-talk begins by understanding what she is experiencing—either low confidence or a recent setback that has affected her self-perception and performance.

Being a leader means being aware of your surroundings and attentive to staff and their concerns. Understanding this enables you to offer targeted support and guidance. Emphasizing your team's outstanding skills and achievements boosts staff morale and improves the learning environment. Focus on your team's successes by offering guidance and ongoing support. Show them examples; it will make your staff feel more confident and happier.

Creating a positive team culture requires addressing negative thinking and fostering a supportive environment. Eliminating negative thoughts empowers team members to embrace new challenges with confidence. It inspires everyone to think creatively, boosting our performance and capability to accomplish tasks.

Through open dialogue and mutual encouragement, you serve as a role model, inspiring your team to adopt the same approach. When everyone unites and supports each other, it fosters trust and improves teamwork and job satisfaction. Follow this path to achieve success with your new franchise.

***

Important Points

- To build a good team culture, it's important to recognize and address negative thinking to create a positive and supportive environment.
- In franchising and entrepreneurship, leaders and franchise owners must acknowledge the significant influence of fear and

self-doubt on personal and professional growth.

- Self-doubt can affect your work environment and communication between your staff, damaging trust and rapport with you as a leader.

- Always act when you're in doubt or fear. Never let it stop you.

- Fear stems from the unknown. Educate yourself and learn from industry experts, mentors, and coaches.

- When you are in doubt, think about the alternatives of not taking the action that is almost needed to take your life and career to new heights.

- Fear is a good thing. It helps you expand your potential and where you can take your talents and tap into possibilities that you never knew existed.

Chapter 9:

Leadership- Ongoing Education Practices

"Learning is not attained by chance; it must be sought with ardor and diligence." ~ **Abigail Adams**

Indra Nooyi, former CEO of PepsiCo, enhanced her expertise by attending executive education programs at prestigious institutions such as Yale University. With her passion for learning, those programs kept her on the edge of the latest business strategies, leadership techniques, and emerging technologies. Nooyi used this knowledge to fuel innovation in PepsiCo's products, packaging, and marketing.

Nooyi's proactive learning approach was essential in understanding how consumers were changing. She attended conferences, engaged with experts, and delved into market research to gain insights into the future of the food and beverage industry. With this knowledge, Nooyi spearheaded PepsiCo's 'Performance with Purpose' strategy, prioritizing healthier products, reduced environmental impact, and sustainable growth. This strategic shift led to healthier brands like Naked Juice and Sabra Hummus, a testament to Nooyi's ability to expect and meet consumer demands.

In her memoir, *My Life in Full: Work, Family, and Our Future*, Nooyi wrote. "I wonder why I am wired this way, where my inner compass always tells me to keep pushing on with my job responsibilities, whatever the circumstances." Nooyi's dedication to learning also emphasized talent development at PepsiCo. She introduced leadership development programs and motivated employees to seek educational opportunities for personal growth. Nooyi also stressed the importance of diversity and inclusion, recognizing that a diverse workforce brings many perspectives and ideas to drive innovation and growth. Through investing in employee education and development, Nooyi built a skilled and motivated workforce that contributed to PepsiCo's success.

As a dedicated leader, pursuing ongoing education is beneficial and crucial to your continued success. According to John F. Kennedy, "Leadership and learning are indispensable to each other." By seeking new knowledge and skills, you show your commitment to growth and improvement and set a positive example for your team.

Starting a franchise involves many challenging aspects of running a small business, such as marketing, branding, products and services, procedures, and processes. However, there is one crucial aspect of your success that the franchisor cannot offer: ready-made leadership.

Franchise leadership is unlike any previous professional experience because you will encounter staff with a wide range of skills and distinct needs in the franchise industry. Leading your franchise is up to you; there's no way around it. To become the best leader possible, you must step up and adapt. Indra Nooyi said, "The challenge of the leader is looking around the corner and making the change before it's too late to make the change." Your ability to adapt to these new leadership challenges as a new franchisee determines whether the franchise succeeds or survives.

Research suggests that transformational leadership is ideal for small business strategies. In contrast to transactional leadership, transformational leadership emphasizes team growth and development through an inspiring purpose. The emphasis is on learning, coaching, and mentoring, not rewards and punishments. As leaders, we should promote our growth and empower our team to prioritize ongoing education.

Influential leaders are lifelong learners seeking opportunities for professional development, whether by attending conferences and workshops, taking courses, or engaging in self-directed study. Doing so expands their knowledge and abilities and inspires their team to do the same.

Continuously learning about current trends in the franchising industry is essential to staying informed and improving practices. Peter Drucker once said, "The greatest danger in times of turbulence is not the turbulence; it is to act with yesterday's logic." By staying current on the latest developments, you can ensure that your leadership strategies are relevant and practical.

As an aspiring franchise leader, pursue ongoing learning through multiple avenues. Some options include reading leadership management books, studying trends, attending webinars and tradeshows, seeking mentorship, engaging in peer groups or networking events, and attending workshops and seminars.

More than anything else, to support your studies and growth, a growth mindset is the key to lifelong learning for leaders. Author and psychologist Carol Dweck stated, "Becoming is better than being." By embracing a growth mindset toward learning, you set yourself up to handle challenges, persist through setbacks, and understand that all efforts, big or small, lead to mastery and business success. Viewing your skills and abilities as ever-changing and growing rather than staying fixated on doing it one way, opens you up to endless opportunities for growth and development.

Continuous education enables you to adapt to the ever-changing leadership landscape. In today's fast-paced business and franchising world, staying ahead of the curve is crucial as technology and business practices grow. You can meet current demands and expect future needs by focusing on learning and growth.

Not only do ongoing education practices benefit you as an individual leader, but they also affect your teams and organization. As Mahatma Gandhi said, "Live as if you were to die tomorrow. Learn as if you were to live forever." Embracing lifelong learning as a leader results in personal and team growth. You motivate others to follow when you prioritize and promote learning and development.

Your commitment to learning should inspire those under your guidance. The impact of your ongoing education should echo throughout your team, changing not only the present but also the future of your organization. As a franchisee and leader, embodying learning is a lifelong journey; you instill curiosity and drive in those around you. It should be contagious. By pursuing knowledge and dedicating yourself to improvement, you create a culture of continuous development within your team.

At the Marigold Academy, our whole mantra is to keep the staff happy and learn to better ourselves, our company, and the staff. They are on the frontline and end-all with happy parents and children. Our teachers constantly need to learn about child development. We require all our teachers and staff members to undergo a certain amount of training every year to ensure they stay on top of the ongoing trends in childcare development and the regulatory landscape. We take this seriously and work hard every day to support our staff in every way possible,

As I delved deeper into ongoing education practices as a leader, I realized its impact on our team and the organization's individual growth and development. While we may not be the largest or most established brand in the US childcare industry, we are well-known for our exceptional quality and over-the-top service to families, children, and staff. It is our differentiator.

Marigold Academy experiences minimal teacher turnover compared to the high turnover rates across the industry. While the rest of the industry struggles to find teachers, Marigold Academy has a waitlist of teachers eager to join and work for us. Marigold Academy's waitlist includes parents keen to secure a spot for their yet-to-be-born child. In today's commercialized childcare industry, we stand above; our strong culture and dedication to learning with a positive and growth mindset sets us apart, helping us rise above.

A positive "can-do" attitude is necessary for franchise leaders to overcome challenges and achieve their goals. A positive attitude transforms. Famous motivational speaker Zig Ziglar once said, "Your attitude, not your aptitude, will determine your altitude." You can overcome and keep moving towards your goals by staying positive and open to learning. Your attitude must remain motivated.

The key to staying motivated is setting small, achievable goals. Antoine de Saint-Exupéry stated, "A goal without a plan is just a wish." When you set concrete and measurable goals and work towards them, you will generate momentum and propel yourself toward success. In my experience, setting clear learning goals and identifying areas where you can improve or study more to be a successful leader is beneficial. This begins by setting specific, measurable goals to guide your learning journey. Also, breaking down more significant goals and objectives into smaller tasks creates a clear path and allows progress to be tracked.

The key to long-term success lies in working toward your goals. However, setting goals alone is not enough because it requires ongoing practice as a habit. As Tony Robbins said, "It's not what we do once in a while that shapes our lives, but what we do consistently." Continuous improvement gives you an edge over your competitors.

In a world that's changing, the winners are the ones who learn and adapt. The only constant in life is change. Keep wanting to learn, set big and small goals, and you'll be ready for anything. Put your knowledge into practice by implementing new ideas, strategies, and skills. Experiment, reflect on the results, and adjust as needed. With leadership changing constantly, it's important to reflect and adapt. Regularly reflect on your learning experiences and how they affect your leadership effectiveness. Adapt your learning plan as needed to ensure continuous growth and development.

Along with goals, from my experience, building a support system with mentors and role models is vital to your success as a new franchisee. Surrounding yourself with individuals who have navigated the complexities of franchise ownership can provide invaluable insights and guidance.

According to a study by the National Mentoring Partnership, "Mentored businesses are more likely to survive and succeed than those without a mentor." By seeking guidance from these experts, you can learn from their experiences and avoid common pitfalls.

Our teams are always there to support and mentor new staff members and franchisees, providing guidance and help every step of the way. Ask questions, be willing to learn, and keep an open mind; that's how to succeed. Learning from those who have overcome similar challenges can benefit new franchisees.

I believe in mentors, humbling myself, and studying under another leadership mentor, all to better myself and do everything I can to be the best leader, father, and husband I can be. Mentors like me can provide firsthand knowledge of the specific obstacles you may encounter and offer practical solutions. Entrepreneur and motivational speaker Jim Rohn once said, "You are the average of the five people you spend the most time with." Surrounding yourself with thriving franchisees boosts your chances of succeeding.

Mentors and role models can help you navigate the dynamic landscape of the franchise industry. As markets evolve and consumer preferences change, guidance from experienced individuals can help you adapt and thrive in challenging environments. By heeding the advice of those who have weathered similar storms, you can position yourself as a resilient and agile leader in the competitive franchise marketplace.

As you continue your journey as a new franchisee, valuing continuous learning and your support system becomes clear. A robust support system can help you develop your leadership skills. By observing the strategies and practices of experienced franchise owners, you can refine your leadership style and approach. Former CEO of General Electric, Jack Welch said, "Before you are a leader, success is all about growing yourself. When you become a leader, success is all about growing others." By learning from those who have successfully led their franchises, you can cultivate the skills to inspire and motivate your team towards success.

By recognizing the support of experienced individuals, you can boost your leadership skills and have more confidence in your decision-making. While navigating the complexities of franchising, remember the strength of a supportive community that encourages you to achieve your objectives. This is the Marigold Academy way.

***

Important Points

- Mentors and role models can help you navigate the dynamic landscape of the franchise industry.
- To stay informed and improve practices, continuously learning about current trends in the franchising industry is essential.
- Following the leads of those who have accomplished their goals before us is the key to succeeding. As a dedicated leader, studying someone else and pursuing ongoing education is not just beneficial; it's crucial to your continued success.

Chapter 10:

Networking-Invisible Marketing Machine

"The aim of marketing is to know and understand the customer so well the product or service fits him and sells itself." ~ **Peter Drucker**

John Mackey and Renee Lawson Hardy, driven by their unwavering passion for natural and organic foods, founded Whole Foods in 1980 in Austin, Texas. Such foods were still emerging in the mainstream market. They started with a small health food store named SaferWay, a clever twist on the popular supermarket chain Safeway. Later, they joined forces with Craig Weller and Mark Skiles, owners of Clarksville Natural Grocery, to open the first Whole Foods Market. The store gained popularity with a workforce of just 19 people because of its unique offering of high-quality, natural, and organic products. Their strategic use of invisible marketing further amplified this success.

Their unique marketing approach influenced Whole Foods, 'invisiBio.' This strategy, rooted in transparency, authenticity, and community building, sets them apart. Instead of traditional advertising, Whole Foods Market fostered a sense of community around their brand. They invited customers to learn about product sourcing, advocated for sustainable practices, and maintained quality standards. The company's dedication to these principles struck a chord with many consumers who prioritized health and sustainability, paving the way for their ongoing success.

Under Mackey's leadership, Whole Foods Market has not only become a beloved organic grocery chain but also a pioneer in invisible marketing through their content strategy. At the heart of this strategy is their blog, a platform where they share valuable information that aligns with their brand values and customer interests. The blog covers a wide range of topics, from recipes and nutrition advice to wellness tips and sustainable living ideas. This approach achieves multiple marketing goals without the overt 'selling' often associated with traditional marketing. Whole Foods reinforces its health-and-sustainability-focused brand image by offering free, high-quality content, educating customers, and increasing appreciation for its products. This strategy builds a community among health-conscious consumers and positions Whole Foods as a trusted authority, often leading to increased customer loyalty and sales.

Whole Foods boosted its website traffic by creating regular, relevant content that made it more visible on search engines. Their blog content offered shareable material on social media, increasing their reach. Without being obvious, their recipes didn't advertise any products.

The success of this approach relied on enhancing customers' lives, not just making sales. When individuals discover helpful content on the Whole Foods blog, they link those positive emotions to the brand. This goodwill often translates into customer loyalty and increased sales without feeling like traditional marketing.

Whole Foods' strategy exemplifies the effectiveness of invisible marketing. By prioritizing customer education and value, their marketing approach generates sales and cultivates a favorable brand perception. This method has helped Whole Foods establish itself as more than just a grocery store—it is a lifestyle brand committed to health and sustainability.

Franchising is a business model where a franchisee buys the right to use a successful business concept and operates it under a licensed trademark. Networking with successful individuals and building meaningful connections can benefit franchisees in several ways. Networking can provide opportunities to learn from the experiences of other successful entrepreneurs and gain valuable insights into the industry.

Building meaningful connections can help franchisees build trust and credibility, leading to more business opportunities and partnerships. Plus, by networking, you, as a new franchisee, can benefit from finding mentorship and guidance, which can be invaluable. Therefore, networking and building meaningful connections are essential skills for franchise success.

When I first transitioned into childcare with Marigold Academy and franchising, I knew one of the first things our small business needed to do was to get our name out there. The more you get the word out and communicate your services and values, the more attention your new business attracts and the more potential customers you bring in. Simon Sinek said, "People don't buy what you do; they buy why you do it." Positive word-of-mouth spread within the community once we implemented our comprehensive age-appropriate curriculums, enhanced health and safety procedures, and provided exceptional care to children, parents, and staff. It was a giant networking boost for the company. More parents heard about our key differentiators they could resonate with, and soon, we started getting increased inquiries, hence building our backlog and waitlist for enrollment.

But it's not always the loudest brands that gain the most attention. When you think about it, a person sees enormous content throughout the day. Brand advertisements inundate us on various platforms, such as social media, email drip campaigns, phone calls, text messages, and more, all attempting to convince us to notice and purchase from them. Starting as an emerging franchise brand, Marigold Academy had to promote its services without disrupting parents and staff. The main point was to realize the potential of referrals and make the most of our network connections.

As a leader and new franchisee, it's crucial to define your networking goals. Before diving into your company's marketing strategy or engaging with potential contacts, establish clear networking goals. Understanding your networking goals and aligning your strategy with your objectives is a key to successful networking.

As part of your networking efforts, show genuine interest in the people you're networking with. I often meet with former CEOs, executives, old colleagues, and friends for casual meetups. My willingness to stay in touch with other influential individuals builds trust, and I have access to their wealth of knowledge and experience.

Researching the right people and merging your interests with them will require effort and due diligence. This way, you can rise above the crowd and make yourself visible to those you're networking with. Leadership author Brene Brown said, "Courage starts with showing up and letting ourselves be seen." There is nothing like showing genuine interest in being there with other people. Instead of focusing only on what benefits you, you can switch gears and learn more about their interests, goals, and dreams.

When we show empathy and ask questions, we create a connection that leads to meaningful relationships. But remember, networking isn't just about business connections—it's about building lasting relationships. It's about delivering your message without beating everyone over the head with it.

Invisible marketing accomplishes all of this, so I want to show you how it works and how it can benefit your new franchise business.

Invisible marketing means promoting your brand without being too obvious. I often use social media platforms like Facebook, Instagram, and LinkedIn to promote Marigold Academy. I teach the viewers about our successful strategies and approaches. I implement social media outreach and maintain the invisible marketing strategy by motivating others to produce and distribute our brand-related content, such as reviews, testimonials, or social media posts. By utilizing this genuine content, your franchise business can establish trust and credibility and promote its brand without a significant financial investment.

We celebrate our success via these platforms to spread awareness and create a healthy, positive tone for our brand and mission. People have reached out to us expressing interest in becoming franchisees because they have noticed our successful work, proven methods, ongoing projects, and achievements.

It's marketing that doesn't feel icky like direct sales. Invisible marketing creates unseen influences that affect how people see your brand. It's about sharing your story subtly without looking salesy. Seth Godin said, "Marketing is no longer about the stuff you make but about the stories you tell."

So, imagine you're strolling through your city and want to sit down and relax after a while. As you turn a corner, you see two sandwich shops. They've got the same products, but one place has outdoor seating, and the other doesn't. And that made you go with the first option. Why is that?

With outdoor seating, the shop made its customers more visible to passersby like yourself. It was inviting and invisible marketing at its best. Those eating outside then became the shop's "representatives." It's a low-key way of promoting their sandwiches, drawing you in. That's an unseen impact. While the idea of unseen marketing is simple, there are key rules to follow for it to be effective. At Marigold Academy, I have discovered there are two rules to this for invisible marketing:

A Parent and Staff-Centric Approach is the Key to Winning in Marigold Academy Franchise.

Understanding your parents and staff is essential before employing invisible marketing techniques. A well-kept customer database is a tool you can leverage to gain information and identify trends. Done periodically, you can have a fool-proof marketing strategy to boost your chances of hitting your goals. With the Marigold Academy franchise, know what makes parents and staff tick, which brings us to our next invisible marketing must-have.

Establishing a Sincere Connection with Your Customers.

According to Harvard University, emotions dominate over 90 percent of consumer purchase decisions, as discovered in their research on the subconscious mind. Apart from the key attributes of a company's services, when people find an emotional connection with a brand, they don't even consider other competitors. At Marigold Academy, our parents and staff are central to our operations and process, as we focus on supporting and building solid relationships while taking the best care of their children. So, how do you win the hearts of your parents and staff?

Start by determining your parents' and staffs' emotions about your brand. Being aware of how your parents and staff behave towards your services enables you to determine which emotions to focus on or evoke in your invisible marketing campaign.

Since the invisible marketing machine is a concept that focuses on the idea that a business can promote itself through relationship building and networking, franchising is a business model that works well with it. You, as a new franchisee, operate under our franchisor's brand, systems, and support. This allows you and our brand to expand by granting others the right to use our business model, and operational processes.

When you combine these two strategies, your business can leverage the network and influence of other business partners to promote it further and expand its reach. New franchisees, for example, can use their local networks to market and promote the business, while we, as the franchisor, can provide support, resources, and expertise to help you succeed.

Combining the invisible marketing machine and franchising allows businesses to tap into the power of relationships and leverage the reach and influence of their network to grow their customer base and expand their business.

Networking Alliances for Franchisees.

Building alliances with complementary businesses can be beneficial for growing your franchise. As you build your network, nurturing these relationships over time is essential to ensure both companies benefit from the partnership. Providing value to your network is vital to maintaining these relationships and can lead to new opportunities. Unobtrusive marketing tactics can help you reach a wider audience without appearing spammy or pushy. In contrast, a subtle brand presence in networking can help you establish trust and credibility with potential partners and families in the community.

By building alliances with complementary and competing businesses, you can offer corresponding products or services to create synergies that benefit both parties. For example, as a childcare center, you can coordinate after-school tutoring or reading and story time in coordinated partnership promotions with other area children-related businesses. This relationship allows each business to offer its families a more comprehensive suite of services without needing to provide everything in-house.

Nurturing relationships over time and investing time and resources into these partnerships could involve regular communication, joint marketing efforts, or collaborative projects. The aim is to create a situation where both businesses benefit more by working together than they could on their own.

Building successful business relationships involves consistently providing value through useful information, sharing opportunities, or helping your partners solve problems. By sharing stories and examples, you strengthen your relationships and increase the likelihood that you'll be top-of-mind when new opportunities arise.

Instead of aggressive marketing, try incorporating unobtrusive tactics into your franchise marketing plan to connect naturally with your audience.

The perception and presentation of a brand in professional and social networks contribute to a subtle brand presence in networking. This covers the design and content of a company's website, social media profiles, and other online platforms, as well as how employees and partners portray themselves and their work in networking events and discussions. A subtle brand presence sets a company apart from competitors, builds trust and credibility, and reinforces brand values and messaging. Author Seth Godin said, "Invisible marketing is the art of making something visible without being visible."

Invisible marketing doesn't mean being unnoticed. It's the art of creating a brand presence that subtly influences decision-making processes, leaving an impression without overt advertising. By understanding the psychology of consumer behavior, businesses can craft strategies that resonate with their audience on a deeper, more subconscious level.

A practical approach in invisible marketing involves creating experiential moments that leave an impression. Instead of overwhelming consumers with conventional advertising, brands can concentrate on creating experiences that seamlessly blend into their everyday routines. Motivate your happy customers to spread the word about their positive experiences with friends, family, and colleagues, resulting in natural brand promotion and referrals.

As a childcare center, you can promote a child's growth through documented learning milestones, which can be a powerful keepsake for the parents and staff. It gets everyone involved, and they feel included, making it a memorable experience. One possibility is to arrange surprise pop-up events, an end-of-summer carnival, or a Halloween parade that brings families together to celebrate, bringing joy to parents and staff.

Remember, authenticity is the unsung champion of covert marketing. Aligning your brand with your consumers' values and beliefs will make your franchise valuable in your community. My wife and I keep our eyes and ears focused on our parents, children, operations, and how we present our story to the community. It is the crux of our business to build a trustworthy childcare center that is trusted throughout our communities.

Brands prioritizing social responsibility, sustainability, or community engagement can establish lasting, authentic connections. Letting actions speak louder than words is crucial for the brand's authenticity to be evident in all areas.

The art of storytelling is a powerful and subtle tool in invisible marketing to foster authenticity in your franchise. By revealing your franchise stories, your brand can establish connections with your audience. Businesses can remain in peoples' awareness by using behind-the-scenes information, relatable stories, and frequent updates.

***

Important Points

- The art of storytelling is a powerful and subtle tool in invisible marketing to foster authenticity.
- An effective approach in invisible marketing involves creating experiential moments that leave an impression.
- The perception and presentation of a brand in professional and social networks contribute to a subtle brand presence in networking.
- Networking can provide opportunities to learn from the experiences of other successful entrepreneurs and gain valuable insights into the industry.
- Building meaningful connections can help franchisees build trust and credibility, leading to more business opportunities and partnerships.

Phase III: Legacy

Chapter 11:

Marigold Commitment

"The deepest form of self-fulfillment is found in selfless giving - for in elevating others, we elevate our own spirits."
~ Jay Shah

In 2013, the Malala Fund came into existence with a strong connection to the extraordinary life journey of Malala Yousafzai. Malala, born on July 12, 1997, hails from Mingora, Pakistan. Since she was young, she campaigned for girls' education in the Swat Valley, where the Taliban had prohibited girls from going to school. Ziauddin Yousafzai, her father, was an educator and a firm proponent of education. He operated a school for girls in their hometown. Malala Yousafzai, a Nobel laureate, and her father are prominent advocates for girls' education worldwide. The primary goal is to provide girls in developing countries and regions affected by conflict or disaster with 12 years of free, secure, and high-quality education, focusing on overcoming barriers to girls' secondary education.

Malala gained international recognition in early 2009, when at just 11 years old, she wrote a blog for BBC Urdu using a fake name. In her blog, she documented her life under Taliban rule and her thoughts on promoting education for girls. The world took notice of her brave voice and advocacy. Yet, her activism also made her vulnerable. On October 9, 2012, a Taliban gunman shot Malala in the head while riding a bus home from school. Astonishingly, she survived the assassination attempt, and they flew her to the United Kingdom for medical care. The attack led to a worldwide surge of support and shed more light on girls' education.

Malala and her father founded the Malala Fund in 2013 to continue the fight for girls' education. The organization prioritizes empowering girls, pushing for policy reforms, and funding education initiatives to ensure for girls, especially in conflict- and poverty-stricken areas. Since its establishment, the Malala Fund has dedicated itself to working with partners in various countries to create opportunities for girls to receive an education and take on leadership roles. Malala continues to be a global symbol of courage and resilience, advocating for education and women's rights worldwide. They awarded her the Nobel Peace Prize in 2014, making her the youngest-ever laureate.

To achieve its goals, the Malala Fund uses four primary strategies. First, it engages with governments and organizations to reform policies that create barriers to girls' education. Second, It assists and uplifts a network of local education activists in countries including Afghanistan, Brazil, India, Lebanon, Nigeria, Pakistan, and Turkey. Third, it provides platforms for girls to share their stories and advocate for their educational rights. Finally, it funds research to identify and overcome barriers to girls' education.

Today, the Malala Fund has had a significant global impact, from boosting girls' enrollment in secondary schools to advocating for increased funding for higher education. Its quick reaction to crises affecting girls' education was clear during the COVID-19 pandemic. Through its multi-faceted approach combining advocacy, grassroots support, and awareness campaigns, the Fund strives to create a world where every girl can learn and lead, fostering individual empowerment and societal progress.

Bill Gates once said, "Effective philanthropy requires a lot of time and creativity—the same skills and focus that building a business requires." Successful franchising hinges on building a powerful community of franchisees who become brand ambassadors and cultivate relationships with their local communities. Several franchise brands take an extra step by seeking to improve lives in communities through philanthropy and charitable giving.

Several brands have grown and integrated charitable initiatives into their business models. These companies have discovered that giving back benefits to those in need strongly connects with consumers. By aligning their products or services with meaningful causes, brands establish emotional connections with customers who value and endorse socially responsible businesses.

For instance, let's look at TOMS Shoes. Their "One for One" model involves donating a pair of shoes for every pair sold and plays a crucial role in the company's rapid market share growth. Patagonia and their support for environmental causes, creating a devoted customer base. Also, through collaborations with UNICEF and Save the Children, IKEA strengthened its worldwide reputation by implementing various sustainability initiatives. Starbucks has strengthened its brand by prioritizing ethical sourcing, community service, and employee education.

These initiatives often lead to positive media coverage, word-of-mouth marketing, and increased customer loyalty. Charitable efforts can boost employee morale and attract top talent who want to work for companies with strong values. As consumers become increasingly conscious of social and environmental issues, brands that show genuine commitment to making a positive impact often see improved sales, enhanced reputation, and long-term sustainability.

Today's consumers consider brand values and a business's commitment to sustainability and social responsibility when making purchasing decisions. The 2019 Aflac Corporate Responsibility Survey found that 77% of consumers prioritize purchasing from companies dedicated to bettering the world, while 73% of investors consider efforts to improve the environment and society when making investment choices. Franchise brands prioritizing charitable causes and community giving are more likely to be favored by customers. When comparing franchise opportunities, a company's philanthropy efforts can be crucial for franchisees in the long term.

The comprehensive approach to charity, community involvement, and project support can give the new franchise owner an edge in their local territory. The franchisee can boost their reputation and attract customers by establishing collaborations with organizations and foundations and associating with a charitable brand. Franchise brands that show how purpose and profit can coexist, are a strong investment opportunity.

For over a decade, my wife and I have supported charitable foundations and contributed to giving back. As Marigold Academy has flourished, so has our ability to create meaningful change. From its inception, a singular mission has driven Marigold Academy: to uplift children and families across all communities we touch. Giving back is investing time, resources, and expertise to advance causes greater than ourselves. Our holistic approach culminated in creating our charitable foundation, Marigold Commitment. Marigold Commitment focuses on three critical pillars:

- **Education and Child Development**: Nurturing young minds and fostering growth.
- **Health and Nutrition:** Ensuring the physical well-being of community members.
- **Poverty Alleviation and Community Development:** Building resilient, thriving neighborhoods.

Through these interconnected areas, we strive to create lasting, positive change. We're not just giving back; we're sowing seeds of hope and opportunity, cultivating a brighter future for all.

Marigold Academy embodies our philosophy of profit with purpose. We dedicate a portion of our proceeds to selected charities, reflecting our focus on creating positive societal impact rather than maximizing profits. Our mission is to address pressing social issues and improve lives through strategic philanthropy. Charity is about giving resources and money to those in need. Volunteerism requires time and effort to assist others through direct engagement. Giving Back encompasses various dimensions, including:

- **Philanthropy**: Strategic donations and investments in causes to catalyze lasting societal improvements.
- **Volunteerism:** Dedicating time and effort to help those in need or contributing to a community.
- **Skills-based volunteering**: Using professional expertise to make a meaningful impact.
- **Advocacy:** Using one's voice to raise awareness and drive positive change.
- **Community engagement**: Participation in local initiatives to build stronger, more resilient communities.

Winston Churchill said, "We make a living by what we get, but we make a life by what we give." Through our ongoing philanthropic efforts, I've witnessed firsthand that collective action and generosity catalyze lasting positive change. By uniting in solidarity and pursuing common goals to help children worldwide, we make a lasting impact, leaving a mark for future generations. At Marigold Commitment, we believe children and education are the cornerstones of a brighter future. We partner with well-regarded organizations, including Children International, ChildFund International, and Save the Children, to affirm this belief. The tireless efforts of these organizations aim to give children and youth a healthy beginning, cultivate nurturing environments for their development, and enable them to bring about enduring change in their lives and communities.

We handpick our partner organizations based on shared values and proven impact. As leaders, we conduct thorough research to ensure our chosen charities align with our mission and the causes we believe in. Our focus is on global non-profits that provide essential services to underprivileged children. These organizations aim to ease poverty through healthcare, education, and critical support services. We prioritize charities committed to improving the lives of children and families worldwide, in marginalized and impoverished communities. The key areas we support include education initiatives to empower children and break the cycle of poverty, healthcare programs for vulnerable populations, child protection and advocacy for children's rights, and emergency response for children affected by conflicts, natural disasters, and diseases.

Children are the most vulnerable in crisis, requiring proper support and necessities to achieve their full potential. At Marigold Commitment, we want to equip children in need with the resources and capacity to improve their lives and become responsible young adults and leaders within their communities.

By partnering with these committed charities, we strive to ensure every child has access to quality education, healthcare, and a safe environment for growth and development. Our support aims to break the cycle of poverty and empower children to shape a brighter future for themselves and their communities. We believe in the transformative power of investing in youth. Our collective efforts can have a long-lasting impact on the lives of many children, empowering them to dream big and realize their capabilities.

Marigold Commitment also recognizes the vital importance of health and nutrition for children and families in underserved communities. We address these critical issues by supporting renowned charities like the Task Force for Global Health, St. Jude Children's Research Hospital, and MAP International.

Our support focuses on three key areas: public health advancement, pediatric healthcare, and resource distribution. We back initiatives that improve global health outcomes, advance public health knowledge and medical research to overcome life-threatening conditions, and ensure access to quality healthcare for all children, regardless of their financial circumstances.

Supporting these organizations enables us to tackle major health issues impacting entire populations. This includes supporting public health research, developing skilled health workforces, and addressing global health challenges such as infectious diseases and vaccine distribution. We help deliver crucial medicines and health supplies to needy communities, making a tangible difference in peoples' lives.

Marigold Commitment aims to create a world where every child and family has access to the health resources and nutrition necessary to thrive regardless of their situation. Our goal is to create a future where good health is accessible to all, not just a privilege for a select few. Our commitment to ending child poverty and impoverished families has led us to develop a strong charitable initiative and find organizations that mirror it. To break the poverty cycle and build resilient communities, it is essential to have a multifaceted strategy. To tackle these complicated issues, we support renowned charities like Sewa International, CARE, and Direct Relief.

Marigold Academy partners with charities that uplift those in need, support local communities, and implement projects for marginalized groups. These organizations focus on comprehensive development initiatives, including family services, child welfare, refugee support, women's empowerment, and health education. They also prioritize disaster relief and rehabilitation efforts.

Vignette: Personal Note from Kruti Shah

Marigold Commitment is all about giving back to the community and organizations so that the children and teachers have what they need and the support to grow. In tandem with Marigold Commitment, Marigold Academy provides a great place where children feel like they are at a second home— where they feel comfortable, safe, inspired, happy, and excited to be there. We wanted a place where children could thrive, learn, and grow, giving the greatest blessing to everyone, especially to the community of families. This is what we're passionate about.

A key emphasis is saving lives and eradicating global poverty, focusing on empowering women and girls. These charities recognize equal rights and opportunities are fundamental to fostering social justice and building prosperous communities. They design their programs to enhance the well-being of individuals affected by poverty or emergencies, providing support regardless of political affiliation, religion, ethnicity, or the ability to pay.

Marigold Commitment cares about empowering women and girls, improving access to education and healthcare, and creating economic opportunities for marginalized communities. We help communities overcome challenges and build a brighter future by supporting these initiatives. Our partnerships prioritize emergency preparedness, disaster response, and disease prevention and treatment, addressing the unique needs of the world's most vulnerable populations.

South African computer scientist and professor Joan Marques said, "It's easier to take than to give. It's nobler to give than to take. The thrill of taking lasts a day. The thrill of giving lasts a lifetime." New franchisees can support charitable initiatives to grow their businesses for several reasons. Charitable efforts help build a positive reputation in the local community, fostering goodwill and customer loyalty while also aligning the franchisee with the broader brand values and mission. These initiatives provide excellent networking opportunities, connecting franchisees with potential families, parents, partners, and community leaders. Moreover, they can boost employee morale and engagement, leading to better retention and productivity.

Supporting local causes often results in positive media coverage and increased visibility for the business, attracting consumers who prefer to support socially responsible companies. While charitable donations can offer tax advantages, the primary benefits lie in differentiation from competitors and the personal fulfillment that comes from contributing to worthy causes.

Building strong community ties through charitable work contributes to the long-term sustainability and success of the franchise. It allows new franchisees to grow their business and affect their community.

At Marigold Commitment, we have adopted a strategic approach to choosing and supporting charities and initiatives that align with our mission and values. We conduct research and due diligence to identify organizations with a proven track record of creating positive, measurable impact in education, health, poverty alleviation, and community development.

We will continue seeking charities with strong leadership, financial transparency, and a commitment to sustainable, long-term solutions. By taking a holistic, partnership-based approach to support various charities, Marigold Commitment aims to create a multiplier effect, amplifying the impact of our collective efforts and bringing us closer to our vision of a world where every child and every community can thrive.

Chapter 12:

Leaving a Lasting Legacy-Why

"The things you do for yourself are gone when you are gone, but the things you do for others remain as your legacy." ~ **Kalu Ndukwe Kalu**

With a $600 loan, David and Barbara Green launched their home-based miniature picture frame venture in 1970. The birth of Hobby Lobby occurred when two years later the fledgling enterprise opened a 300-square-foot store in Oklahoma City. With over 1,000 stores, Hobby Lobby is now the world's largest privately owned arts-and-crafts retailer, employing over 46,000 people across 48 states. Hobby Lobby is mainly an arts-and-crafts store, but it also offers hobbies, picture framing, jewelry making, fabrics, floral and wedding supplies, cards and party ware, baskets, wearable art, home decor, and holiday merchandise. The corporate headquarters in Oklahoma City now spans over 12 million square feet, encompassing manufacturing, distribution, and an office complex. Hobby Lobby also maintains offices in Hong Kong, Shenzhen, and Yiwu, China. It's hard to imagine starting all of that with just $600, expanding the business, serving customers nationwide, and helping them live a generous and giving life while leaving behind a huge legacy for family.

A key principle guiding me in my CEO and leadership role at the Marigold Academy is intending to leave a lasting legacy for my family. My wife and I believe in having and leaving a legacy for our two daughters. Together, we work towards our goals and make decisions that align with our mission to create a lasting legacy.

We build our legacy on our purpose: to ensure high-quality childcare is available in all communities. We believe children absorb everything around them, both good and bad. Kevin Costner said, "we must stand firm on important principles to set a good example for our children." It is our responsibility as a society to challenge our children from a young age. At Marigold Academy, our focus is on challenging children from a young age, ensuring they receive proper nutrition and safety, and fostering curiosity and learning. Additionally, we give priority to the development of our staff, believing that progress should be based on hard work and ability rather than just circumstances. Philosopher Paul Dirac noted, "Your knowledge is more valuable than degrees." We value people for their character, not just their education or degrees. This approach forms the core of our mission; to affect children's lives and create a lasting, meaningful legacy in childcare and education.

In every business, there are leaders and those who lead. Although we understand we may not have the same level of establishment as other childcare brands in the USA, our exceptional quality and high standards make us stand out. Unlike the industry norm of high staff turnover, we maintain consistent teacher retention. While the rest of the industry struggles to find teachers, Marigold Academy has a waitlist of teachers eager to join us. Parents join Marigold Academy's waitlist before their children are even born. That is a testament to our strong culture and superior care. This reputation is rare in childcare and fundamental to our enduring legacy.

My leadership focuses on motivating our teachers while delivering outstanding childcare and early education. This approach positions us as pioneers and a rising force in the industry. Our success in retaining staff, attracting families, and providing top-tier care shows our unique position in the childcare landscape and our commitment to setting new standards in early childhood education.

Reflecting on the stories of Hobby Lobby and Marigold Academy, it's clear that every one of us is building our legacy daily through our work and community service. You don't need to be a famous tycoon or celebrity to make a meaningful impact; ordinary people often leave behind powerful legacies. If you're questioning your current path and the mark you'll leave on the world, consider the potential impact of becoming a franchisee with us. This opportunity could be a significant step in shaping your legacy. It's worth taking a moment to consider the impact you want to have and the legacy you wish to create. What will your legacy be? How will you use your time and resources to make a positive difference in your community and beyond?

Fostering a culture of support for our teams and staff is a key part of the legacy we aim to build at Marigold Academy. By joining our franchise model, you can instill our company's principles in your staff while shaping the business' direction based on your values. We provide comprehensive training and ongoing support systems, equipping you with the tools to create a nurturing environment for your teachers and promote their career growth.

Friends, family and the teams you lead will remember your legacy. It's crucial to ensure that your impact influences those who contribute to your business' success. By focusing on staff development and creating a supportive work culture, you can build a lasting legacy that extends beyond the walls of your franchise and into the lives of your employees and the families you serve.

At Marigold Academy, our mission is to influence our communities positively. We're committed to helping local areas thrive by partnering with other businesses and creating opportunities for career growth. As a franchise, we believe that building a lasting legacy involves supporting and serving our communities through volunteer work and charitable initiatives. Our Marigold Academy model aims to be remembered not just for the high-quality childcare we provide, but also for the many ways we contribute to community well-being. We strive to create a ripple effect of positive change, ensuring that our presence enhances the lives of families, employees, and the broader community. By focusing on both excellent care and community engagement, we aim to leave a legacy of compassion, growth, and meaningful support in every area we serve.

Leaving a lasting legacy is essential for many reasons. When we live fully, our lives gain more meaning and purpose. Legacy enables us to make a positive impact on future generations. Our actions can motivate others to uphold the same values and principles.

Knowing that our contributions have made a lasting difference and leaving a legacy brings a sense of fulfillment and accomplishment. It's a means for people to be remembered and impact the world. In the world of business, a legacy secures the lasting impact of our efforts, benefiting our loved ones and communities in the future. Prioritizing legacy prompts us to live purposefully, make decisions that align with our long-term objectives and values, and inspires us to pursue greatness.

Building a legacy and giving back to the community are the primary focuses of our franchise model, with profitability as an important but secondary consideration. We believe that by prioritizing positive impact, financial success will naturally follow. However, we recognize we operate in a capitalist society where profitability and cash flow are essential for sustaining your business and entrepreneurial aspirations.

The ability to do good for your family and society in the long term depends on responsible and profitable actions.

It's important to understand that you should view money based on your efforts, not as your primary purpose. While there's a stage in life where earning money is crucial for providing for your family and sustaining yourself, beyond a certain point, it's no longer just about financial gain. As you excel in meaningful endeavors, financial rewards follow. Our philosophy is to strive for excellence in service and community impact, trusting that financial success will be a natural result of these efforts.

Marigold Academy franchising offers a powerful way to create a lasting legacy through business ownership. Our model provides five key benefits for building a generational legacy:

Financial Stability: Our proven business model and established brand increase your chances of success and revenue generation, providing financial security for you and your family.

Established Brand and Systems: You'll benefit from our proven business model and operational systems, giving you a solid foundation for success and growth.

Scalability: Our emerging franchise model allows for efficient expansion to multiple locations, hence increasing your business value and enhancing your family's legacy.

Ongoing Support and Training: We provide comprehensive help to prepare you and future generations for successful business management, helping you navigate entrepreneurship challenges and protect your legacy.

Community Impact: As a Marigold Academy franchise owner, you'll make a lasting difference through children's education, job creation, and local economic contributions, establishing a legacy that goes beyond financial success.

Franchising with Marigold Academy offers unique opportunities and challenges in building a lasting legacy. It is important to emphasize strength and integrity throughout this journey. As you think about this option, it's important to know what our franchise provides, plan for the future when you decide to leave, and concentrate on leaving a meaningful legacy for your family. We take pride in our franchise model and strive to ensure it aligns with your personal values and goals. This alignment is key to the success and longevity of your legacy. By choosing Marigold Academy, you're not just starting a business, but embarking on a journey to create a meaningful impact that can last for generations.

Although the challenges of franchising may feel overwhelming, maintaining your integrity and making ethical decisions will make you stand out. By establishing a solid groundwork for your company, you motivate others and offer encouragement and help to those pursuing their aspirations. Continue moving forward, understanding that your actions can influence lives beyond your imagination.

Expanding your franchise means facing new obstacles that push your determination to the limit. Managing consistency across multiple locations can be daunting, but our systematic process helps you overcome these hurdles. No matter what gets in your way, following the system and staying true to the brand will elevate your schools from the competition. Your determination inspires your team and encourages other entrepreneurs to follow their dreams. Each obstacle you overcome adds to your legacy as a successful and principled franchise owner. Remember, following our proven methods and maintaining brand integrity are key to your growth and success. As you expand, you're not just growing a business; you're building a lasting legacy that inspires others and makes a real difference in your community.

***

Vignette: Personal Note from Gary Occhiogrosso

In franchising, I quickly learned the difference between the work of the business and the business. As a development tool and business model, I believe that franchising is the best or the greatest business model ever created in the history of the United States. Most businesses in the United States are small businesses. Not everybody is Mark Zuckerberg or Elon Musk. In truth, Main Street USA and not Wall Street create the vast majority of GDP in this country. Most individuals running franchises are startup entrepreneurs or might own multi-unit brands. Franchising is perhaps the biggest gateway to self-reliance creating equity and generational wealth.

***

As your franchise grows, focus on balancing expansion with consistency. Face challenges with resilience, seeing them as opportunities for growth. Your ability to lead by example will inspire your team and help you stand out in the industry. This approach shows how perseverance and integrity build a legacy that goes beyond mere business success.

We all want to feel connected to something greater than ourselves. Leaving a legacy means passing on something special to future generations. We can all impact the world through work, family, or community. What we do for a living affects the world—our body of work can leave an impression. It's not just about money but finding meaning in our work.

As CEO of Marigold Academy, a key part of my legacy is helping our franchisees and aspiring entrepreneurs succeed. Sharing the wisdom and knowledge I have gained from lessons learned has led us to where we are, which is, in my mind, a great way to "pay it forward" and help shape the next generation of leaders. We have built our success on guiding principles that focus on understanding and motivating our team, recognizing their strengths and weaknesses, and guiding them toward impactful careers. As you pursue your goals as a franchisee, consider how your actions can influence your team and staff. This approach builds your business and creates a lasting legacy that contributes to a better world. Remember, your role as a leader extends beyond business operations—it's about nurturing talent, inspiring growth, and making a meaningful difference in people's lives.

Franchising with Marigold Academy can be a powerful business strategy, offering significant profit potential and many benefits. Expanding your local brand is one of the major advantages, leveraging the success of our existing business model. However, like any business approach, franchising comes with its own set of challenges alongside its benefits. Building a legacy through franchising requires strength, resilience, and the ability to make tough decisions. To achieve substantial growth and impact through franchising, one must carefully consider and commit to maintaining the quality and values that the franchise brand is known for. It is particularly important to ensure consistency across multiple franchise locations.

Understanding your self-worth and taking calculated risks is crucial to building a lasting legacy for your loved ones. Recognizing your unique value empowers you to make choices aligned with your aspirations. By stepping out of your comfort zone, you open doors to personal growth and fulfillment. This mindset allows you to create a meaningful team environment that impacts others. Your legacy is shaped not just by how you made people feel but by the tangible changes you brought to their lives. Embrace your worth, take bold steps, and unlock the potential for a meaningful life. Remember, your actions and decisions today can create a legacy that inspires and influences others long into the future. By valuing yourself and taking thoughtful risks, you're not just building a business—you're crafting a legacy that can transform lives and leave a lasting, positive impact on your community.

***

Important Points

- Prioritize fostering a supportive culture for your teams and staff as a core part of your legacy development.
- As you grow, balance growth with consistency. Face each obstacle with resilience. Your exemplary leadership will inspire your team and distinguish you from the industry.
- Understanding self-worth and calculated risk-taking is fundamental to creating a lasting legacy for your loved ones.
- Your goal is to leave a positive legacy that extends beyond your lifetime, creating or catalyzing something that benefits future generations and contributes to a better world.

Chapter 13:

Marigold Way-Reflection and Leadership Takeaways

"Your story is the greatest legacy that you will leave to your friends. It's the longest-lasting legacy you will leave to your heirs." ~ **Steve Saint.**

When I chose a different path in my career and life, going against the expectations of those around me, the idea and vision of Marigold Academy became deeply rooted in my heart. The idea burned, and I knew there was no other path in my life that I wanted to pursue. The intensity of the dream about Marigold Academy consumed my thoughts, leaving no room for ignoring it any longer.

This journey has taught me that reaching the pinnacle is not a destination, but an ongoing odyssey fueled by unwavering drive, fierce determination, boundless passion, relentless perseverance, and a clear sense of purpose. As a CEO of Marigold Academy, I can attest that every step of the way is a testament to the power of incremental progress, starting with setting clear goals fueled by an unwavering dedication to yourself, your family, and your business. Each milestone achieved is a celebration of hard work and resilience.

The journey to the top is not a one-time event but a continuous pursuit. Stay committed and motivated, and you will reach your goals. Achieving greatness does not happen overnight. It's about taking small steps every day toward a bigger vision.

It's not about reaching the final destination, but about the transformation you experience while taking daily steps towards your aspirations. Along the way, the wisdom that is acquired fosters gratitude and molds you into an inspiring leader. During the journey, you are shaped, transforming challenges into steppingstones and setbacks into lessons. As you progress, you approach your goals and develop into a more resilient, insightful, and empathetic individual. This personal growth becomes your most precious achievement, far outweighing any tangible success. The path you walk shapes the leader you become, leaving a lasting impact on those around you and creating a legacy that extends beyond mere accomplishments.

As a new franchisee and leader, break your journey into manageable steps. Stay humble and build a supportive network. When I founded Marigold Academy, I put our team and staff first. My vision was to create an unparalleled environment where children, families, parents, and staff felt valued and cared for. Each small step forward has propelled our franchise towards excellence by focusing on this. Remember, the daily acts of care and commitment build an influential organization.

When I founded Marigold Academy, I envisioned success beyond financial gains. Our true measure of achievement lies in our positive impact on children, families, and our staff. We're not just creating a business but nurturing dreams and building legacies for aspiring entrepreneurs.

As CEO, I find profound fulfillment in our community impact. Our franchise isn't just a business model; it's a testament to our dedication to education, growth, and community development. Seeing our team members advance in their careers, watching children thrive in our care, and supporting franchisees as they build their success stories are the real rewards. We're creating a ripple effect of positive change, and that's the heart of Marigold Academy's mission.

With Marigold Academy expanding into multiple locations, our next challenge and goal is clear: thoughtful expansion. We aim to bring quality childcare to more families nationwide, but growth isn't just about numbers. Our focus is on scaling without compromise, ensuring each new location embodies the high standards of care and education that define the Marigold brand. As we expand, we're not just opening centers but extending our commitment to excellence in early childhood development to communities across the country.

Building your legacy with our family and franchise hinges on truly embodying our brand's values, understanding our audience, and honoring our story. As a new franchisee, your authenticity is key. Embrace our franchise's spirit rather than pushing for changes that might clash with our core mission.

Leadership in our franchise demands staying current with industry trends while appreciating our history. This balance ensures that your decisions and direction maintain continuity with our established identity. Remember, you're not just running a business; you're carrying forward a vision and a promise to our community. You create a powerful synergy by aligning your passion with our franchise's mission. This alignment drives success and ensures that every action you take contributes to a legacy that resonates with our values and serves our families for generations to come.

Franchising Marigold Academy is not just about expanding our reach; it is about entrusting others with the brand's legacy and values. Our shared stories of success and challenges always emphasize the importance of mindset and tenacity in achieving our goals. I believe in leading with integrity and setting an example for our teams, teachers, and franchise partners.

As a leader, I lead with empathy and compassion. Those two attributes are not signs of weakness but of true leadership strength and growth. As a new franchisee, it is crucial to prioritize and foster a supportive team culture where everyone feels empowered to contribute their best.

As a Marigold franchise leader, your creativity is key. Bring in fresh ideas while honoring our core values—this balance strengthens our impact on the community. Innovation helps you connect with children and families, serving them in meaningful ways.

Your role is to inspire excellence in your team. Lead with integrity, empathy and compassion, and you'll shape Marigold Academy's future, one center at a time. There's nothing more rewarding than walking into a school buzzing with energy and enthusiasm—a testament to the positive culture we have worked so hard to build.

Your innovative spirit and our established principles create a powerful legacy. It's not just about running a childcare center; it's about nurturing a vibrant community where children thrive, and families feel supported. By focusing on creativity, excellence, and compassion, you're not just leading a franchise, you're fostering an environment where lasting, positive memories are made every day.

It's difficult not to feel a surge of pride as I write this, witnessing my team mirror my dreams and vision, all devoted to achieving excellence. As I walk through our classrooms, I notice that the genuine smiles on the faces of the children and teachers make all the hard work worthwhile. Parents' sincere feedback and heartfelt testimonials inspire me to overcome challenges and strive for improvement in our childcare services. The true purpose lies in creating a lasting impact and nurturing and uplifting the lives of the children we interact with daily.

My dedication to leading with integrity resonates in every decision I make, from selecting franchise partners who share our values to ensuring that every child receives the same level of care, education, and attention regardless of location. My responsibility as a leader is to pursue and drive the business in this positive direction. Empathy and compassion are not just buzzwords at Marigold Academy; they're woven into the fabric of our operations, guiding our interaction with families, staff, and the community at large. Our vision for the franchise extends beyond business success; it is about creating a legacy of excellence and impact that will endure for generations to come.

As Marigold Academy Franchise continues to grow, I am proud that each new location brings us one step closer to fulfilling our mission of widespread quality childcare. We constantly improve through feedback from families and staff, balancing expansion with maintaining high standards.

As Marigold Academy franchise expands, I remain hands-on to ensure our franchisees get the proper support. Authentic leadership is not about giving orders from a distance but about being present, listening, and leading by example. We've fostered a culture of teamwork where everyone's strengths contribute to creating a nurturing environment for children to thrive. This collaborative approach, valuing each team member's input, is the cornerstone of our success and the key to fulfilling our vision of exceptional childcare.

I want to express my gratitude for everyone's dedication and hard work in upholding Marigold Academy's values. Every smile, lesson, and hug you give makes a difference. The vision of the Marigold Academy franchise is that every child, regardless of background or circumstance, has access to quality care and education that would improve their lives. We aim to grow and reach more communities; however, I can't over-emphasize that growth should never come at the cost of compromising our core values. True success is not measured by the number of centers opened, but by our positive impact on children and families. Your dedication is shaping a brighter future for the next generation.

We share a sense of purpose and determination for Marigold Academy's future. We encourage continuous learning and improvement, adapting to meet families' growing needs, and staying true to our commitment to excellence in childcare.

***

Vignette: Personal Note from Kruti Shah

Our vision is all thanks to our children. That is how we got started. After looking at so many daycares, not one of them had the home-away-from-home culture and environment we wanted for our children. So, we created it ourselves, and that started the dream. It wasn't easy—there were plenty of challenges along the way. It required many sacrifices, long working days, and hard work. Finally, when everything fell into place, everything was happening and working out right, it felt surreal. Jay and I felt blessed and overwhelmed with gratitude. We knew we were embarking on something special, all because we wanted the best for our children and realized other parents did too.

***

Reflecting on Marigold Academy's journey, I'm filled with profound gratitude. Our success is not my achievement alone but the result of our collective dedication—our passionate teams, committed franchisees, and the families who've entrusted us with their most precious gifts, their children. My legacy is in ensuring that each of you feels valued and recognized for your crucial role in our mission. Marigold Academy isn't just a childcare center; it's a community where genuine connections flourish between staff, children, families, and our franchise partners.

Every smile, milestone, and word of appreciation fuels my passion and reaffirms my belief in the transformative power of quality childcare. Together, we're not just shaping young minds but nurturing the future, one child at a time. As we continue to grow, let's remember that our strength lies in our unity, shared vision, and unwavering commitment to excellence. Thank you for being the heart and soul of Marigold Academy. Your dedication inspires me daily, and I'm honored to lead such an extraordinary team.

As a leader, my legacy means building a sound foundation that lasts beyond my time. Foundation that keeps our beliefs and mission alive for generations to come. As Benjamin Disraeli said, "The legacy of heroes is the memory of a great name and the inheritance of a great example." The ownership of a Marigold Academy franchise provides a unique opportunity to leave a lasting impact. Seize the chance to establish a business that aligns with your principles, impacts the community, and exemplifies your hard work and vision.

What legacy do you want to leave behind? At Marigold Academy, we build lasting impacts every day through our work in childcare and community service. By joining our franchise, you can create your positive legacy with the support of our proven system.

As an owner, you'll shape your team's values, foster a strong ethical culture, and create an environment where your staff can grow.

Remember, beyond your family and friends, it's your teachers and team who will carry your legacy forward. By impacting those who run your business, you're creating a meaningful and enduring legacy in your community.

As a Marigold Academy franchisee, your legacy will be your impact on the community. We're committed to giving back and creating a sustainable future for families. Owning a Marigold Academy Franchise offers you a path to financial independence and wealth-building for your family. Our proven system makes this possible. Many new franchise owners, like yourself, plan to hand over the business to their children in order to secure their financial future and have a clear plan for leaving the business. By joining Marigold Academy, you're not just starting a business—you're creating a lasting legacy that can benefit your family and community for generations to come.

We're grateful for your unwavering support of Marigold Academy and our mission to nurture young minds. As a new franchisee, we're excited to help you build a transcending legacy for your family while making a difference in children's lives across the nation. This is a legacy you can be proud of.

Welcome aboard, and best wishes for your success.

Jay and Kruti Shah

Marigold Academy

About the Author

Jay Shah

Founder & CEO

Jay Shah is a Founder and CEO of Marigold Academy, a rapidly growing early childhood education franchise known for its commitment to excellence. With his knowledge, expertise, and leadership, Jay has built a successful childcare franchise that provides high-quality early education to children before they enter kindergarten.

Jay's journey embodies the American dream. After immigrating to the United States in 1995, he built an impressive career through determination and dedication to continuous learning. Armed with an Electrical & Computer Engineering degree from Wayne State University and an MBA from Michigan State University, Jay spent 15 years in corporate America, holding diverse positions in engineering, supply chain, operations, and finance.

His entrepreneurial spirit led him to franchise ownership, where he successfully owned and operated four Dunkin' Donuts locations. This experience provided invaluable insights into franchise operations and management. In 2019, Jay transitioned into early childhood education, bringing a unique blend of corporate expertise, franchise experience, and business acumen to the industry.

Drawing from his diverse background, Jay has developed innovative approaches to childcare management and delivery, driven by a deep commitment to making high-quality early education accessible to all communities. His vision extends beyond business success – he believes in empowering professionals to create lasting legacies through entrepreneurship in early education. Through Marigold Academy, Jay partners with motivated individuals who share his commitment to community impact, leveraging his comprehensive understanding of both corporate operations and franchise ownership to guide others in their journey to childcare center ownership.

Kruti Shah

Founder & President

Kruti Shah is a Founder and President of Marigold Academy. Like Jay, Kruti's journey began with humble roots, where she gained invaluable business experience helping with her family's franchise operations from an early age. Kruti has a degree in architecture; however, she has been part of the early education and childcare industry since 2019. Kruti is passionate about children, their well-being, and education. Apart from being involved in overseeing the corporate Marigold Academy locations, Kruti remains actively involved in her community, regularly volunteering at her daughters' elementary school. Her hands-on experience as both an educator and a parent brings an invaluable perspective to Marigold Academy's mission of providing exceptional early childhood education.

About Our Franchising Opportunity

For 30 years, Marigold Academy has set the gold standard in early childhood education. Our comprehensive curriculum is thoughtfully designed to create a seamless learning journey from infancy through pre-K. Each program builds upon the previous one, developing essential academic, social, and emotional skills that prepare children for kindergarten success.

Our experienced educators create engaging environments where children develop a natural love for learning. From early literacy and STEM exploration to social skills and creative expression, we nurture every aspect of your child's development.

To learn more about Marigold Academy, please visit us at: https://marigoldacademy.com/franchising

www.ingramcontent.com/pod-product-compliance
Lightning Source LLC
Chambersburg PA
CBHW060321050426
42449CB00011B/2588